What people are saying about

The Water Witch

Jessica Howard's *The Water Witch* is a uniq exploration of all things water. This bo... historical information – such as the cultural importance of water throughout the ancient world – as well as practical tools for connecting with this element. Each chapter includes practical exercises designed to help the reader embody their own inner water witch. As a long time devotee of water magick, I would highly recommend this book to anyone interested in incorporating the element of water into their spiritual practices.
Robin Corak, Author of Moon Books *Persephone: Practicing the Art of Personal Power,* and *Demeter*

Jessica Howard explores the element of water giving a fascinating insight into the history, myth, gods and goddesses, elementals and more. Whatever your preference of bodies of water be it oceans, rivers, lakes, spring, snow, moon rainwater, or all of these and more, Jessica Howard will guide you into introducing them into your magical practices. With practical exercises, spells, rituals, and meditations, this inspiring introduction is perfect for those wishing to embark on a magical journey as a water witch, and in fact any witch will discover something of use in this helpful guide.
Harmonia Saille, Author of *Pagan Portals – Hedge Witchcraft, Hedge Riding,* and *Magic for Hedges Witches*

As a Pisces, married to a Sailor, I pay attention to water in all its manifestations (from ocean to refreshing drink). As a rune magician I am always eager to expand my understanding of the runes. I collect water from different locations for magical purposes, always mindful of the Water Rune: Laguz.

In this book Jessica Howard speaks of water as the 'otherworldly unknown' and she introduces us to the ways of the Water Witch as a knowledge seeker. She introduces water deities (and may I suggest that you also start a list of your own, reflecting your own location or ancestral background?). She also describes scrying methods (the art of inducing a vision by staring at something) and the cleansing of spiritual objects, all using water. If water exerts its magical pull on you, this is a very practical book. Really, it is a diving board for (aspiring) water witches. Treat yourself to an adventure!

Imelda Almqvist, international teacher of Sacred Art and Seiðr, author of four books including *Sacred Art: A Hollow Bone for Spirit* and *Medicine of the Imagination: Dwelling in Possibility (An Impassioned Plea for Fearless Imagination)*

Pagan Portals

The Water Witch

An Introduction to Water Witchcraft

Pagan Portals

The Water Witch

An Introduction to Water Witchcraft

Jessica Howard

MOON
BOOKS

Winchester, UK
Washington, USA

JOHN HUNT PUBLISHING

First published by Moon Books, 2023
Moon Books is an imprint of John Hunt Publishing Ltd., No. 3 East Street, Alresford
Hampshire SO24 9EE, UK
office@jhpbooks.net
www.johnhuntpublishing.com
www.moon-books.net

For distributor details and how to order please visit the 'Ordering' section on our website.

ISBN: 978 1 78535 955 2
978 1 78535 956 9 (ebook)
Library of Congress Control Number: 2021953215

A CIP catalogue record for this book is available from the British Library.

Design: Matthew Greenfield

UK: Printed and bound by CPI Group (UK) Ltd, Croydon, CR0 4YY
Printed in North America by CPI GPS partners

We operate a distinctive and ethical publishing philosophy in
all areas of our business, from our global network of authors to
production and worldwide distribution.

Contents

Chapter 1

What is Water Witchcraft?

For thousands of years water has captured the heart and the imagination. From tales of benevolent spirits that dwell in lakes and ponds, to the ferocious sea monsters that lurk in the depths, history and local folklore is full of tales of the mysterious and otherworldly nature of this element. Many creation myths stem from the waters that surround us, and water God's, Goddesses and spirits are plenty. This element of mystery, the otherworldly unknown, is one of the many reasons people are drawn to water witchcraft. In the still waters of ponds and lakes we find a mirror to ourselves, and in the rising and the falling of the tides we see how our own fortunes wax and wane.

Water witchcraft is magic performed primarily with the element of water. This isn't to say that the water witch works exclusively with the element of water (although some do), but they work with it more so than the other elements. A water witch will often incorporate other elements into their practice to strengthen their works (such as using herbs and crystals, generally associated with the element of earth, or candles which are associated with the element of fire). But the element of water is the one they connect most closely with, and this fuels their practice.

This book is intended to be an overview or an introduction to water witchcraft. There is so much information that to cover it in one book, especially in any sort of depth, would be impossible. However, this book should give you an insight into the way of the water witch, and help you bring the element of water into your own practice. I have always been quite practical in my application of magic. I will pull tarot cards as I'm sitting at my desk checking my emails, or stop to say a quick blessing at my shrine before heading out to get the shopping done. I've never been one for intricate rituals or fancy tools. However, I know water witches whose practices are more focused around water worship in a reverent and ritualistic sense, and for whom performing rituals and magic is an important part of their practice. Then there are those who don't perform any sort of magic but prefer to just connect with bodies of water and spirits and let those guide them. Out of everything I've written in this book, by far the most important thing is your connection to the element of water and how you experience it. Exactly how you do this is up to you; you may have zero interest in working with animal guides but work with two or three deities. The idea of working with the tides or astrological correspondences may be something that just doesn't excite you but you are really interested in meditation. Maybe your real passion is making different types of sprays, perfumes, waters, and healing remedies – there is no reason you can't keep this as a focus and just use the energy of water to enhance your workings and guide you.

There is no one 'right way' when it comes to water witchcraft. There are no set rules, no creeds, no one organized group which dictates 'you must do x, y, and z to call yourself a water witch'. Everything in this book is my interpretation of it. I may say that I associate creativity with the element of water and so creativity features heavily throughout my practice, but that might not be for you. I may say that a water witch is a knowledge seeker and one of the ways to gain this knowledge is through journeying, but you may have zero interest in journeying. One thing that I have learned from talking with others who practice water witchcraft is that no-one practices exactly the same. The element of water does have some core associations, and feeling an affinity with these is one of the reasons many people may choose a path that could be called water witchcraft. But never feel afraid to forge your own path; just like the element of water, our practices can be fluid and ever changing.

The element of water has many different positive associations, but water can also be destructive; from floods to tidal waves, it has the power to destroy as well as create. Sometimes this is necessary to make way for new possibilities and growth. Most water witches do not shy away from this, and work with the element of water to help them overcome the challenges they face and acknowledge that the difficult times are a chance for learning and growth. Acknowledging the more negative associations of not just the elements, but ourselves, can be difficult, but it is important to do so. Through this exploration, we can turn weakness into strength, be better prepared to manage through the difficult periods, and bring peace and balance into our lives.

So, what is the element of water associated with? Below is just a brief list of some of the most common associations of this element. Remember, what matters the most is how you experience it.

- Emotions and the emotional self
- The Goddess
- Healing
- Dreamwork
- Divination
- Moon Magic
- Spirit work
- Knowledge and wisdom
- Cleansing and purification
- Psychic abilities and intuition
- Birth, death, and the cycles of life
- The otherworld
- Femininity
- Love, beauty, compassion, and forgiveness

I also feel that creativity is very much intertwined with the element of water. Creativity is most commonly associated with the element of air, and so this is an example as to where I personally deviate from the norm. I've always been passionate about writing, and when I'm sitting at my desk or with a notebook in hand, I can almost feel the words flowing like water through a river. Think of the term 'divine inspiration'; with this element being closely connected to the Goddess and the otherworld, I can't help but feel a divine creative inspiration when I'm working with the element of water. Whilst it isn't a common attribute of the water element, it is a part of my experience when working with water, and so features heavily in my own path.

The Water Witch

Before you go any further, think about why you are here; what is it that has drawn you to water witchcraft? Are you interested in finding out more about water witchcraft specifically, or maybe you just want to learn more about this element to balance it alongside the other elements in your practice?

Many witches like to keep a journal to record their thoughts, ideas, and practices. If you don't have one, I recommend finding one you can use at least for the duration of this book. Your journal can be a great tool in helping you learn, grow, and reflect.

Once you have found your journal, just take a few minutes to write about what being a water witch means to you. You can write as much or as little as you want – this is your chance to define what it is that you want out of this path.

Personally, there are several reasons as to why I follow the path of a water witch. The main ones are to help with healing, knowledge seeking, transformation, creativity, and intuitive practice. Below I have just written a little bit on what each means to me and how I believe we can use water energies to achieve them, to give you an idea as to how you may start defining your own path.

Healing

The ability to heal is very important to me. As one of the main associations of the element of water, the path of the water witch allows me to more easily connect with the energies needed to heal. With emotions being so strongly associated with the element of water, I believe that the water witch's expertise lies more in emotional and spiritual healing as opposed to physical healing. Our emotional and spiritual health can have an impact on our physical health though, and so it is good practice to make sure we are taking care of ourselves in these areas as we would our physical bodies.

Healing can take many forms, and oftentimes healing can be used as a chance to celebrate our strengths, understand and work on our weaknesses, and grow as people. Through this growth we can find balance and understanding, and gain a deeper awareness of the world around us.

We can practice healing by using enchanted waters to wash ourselves with or bath in, or to drink. Shells can be used as you would crystals, herbs can be incorporated into washes, and deities and spirits called upon to aid in our healing. We can use the flowing of the rivers to carry away that which causes us harm and protect ourselves from further damage. Cleansing and purification is one of the most prominent associations of the element of water and we can use this to help prevent harmful energies from building up and negatively impacting us. As the saying goes, prevention is better than cure.

Knowledge Seeking

As well as healing, I have always considered myself a bit of a 'knowledge seeker'. I'm definitely not the smartest of people but you don't need to be to enjoy learning, and the element of water can aid us in our pursuit of knowledge. The depths of the oceans hold many secrets, and has born life from the beginning of time. We can use water to help us uncover these ancient secrets and this knowledge, to help us gain wisdom and apply those lessons to our everyday life.

There are many different ways in which the element of water can help us. Water has been seen through several different civilizations as a way to the otherworld, and crossing water is often seen as a way to travel from one world to the next. We can use this to help us connect and communicate with those in the otherworld, whether that is through working with water spirits, or through a practice such as journeying.

Divination is another way in which we can open ourselves to receive this knowledge. There is a whole section on divination later on in the book, so I won't go into too much detail here. Similarly, working with animal guides, deities, and ancestors is another way in which we can gain knowledge and learn the lessons that life is trying to teach us. By connecting and working with the element of water, we can learn to understand not just the worlds around us but the worlds within us too.

Transformation

Transformation is another aspect of the element of water that I feel particularly drawn to. I know that sounds odd, as transformation mostly comes through change which is often unintentional. But for me personally, I see transformation as a gateway to self-fulfilment.

As the tides of the sea rise and fall, the element of water governs the cycles of life. This includes the cycle of birth, death, and rebirth, as well as the cycles of joy, suffering, and growth. The water witch does not shy away from any of these phases, understanding that they are necessary. Even the more negative periods are chances for us to reflect, learn from our mistakes, and move forward better than we were before. Only through this transformation can we gain the knowledge and wisdom we seek.

Water is a fluid element, often in motion, and the element itself transforms and adapts to its environment. When it is cold, it freezes. When it warms again, it melts. The element of water can help us understand the need to go with the flow and to adapt without ever losing our sense of self.

Many different cultures, such as the Mesopotamians, have creation myths which teach us how all life sprung from the primordial seas and gave birth to the world. There are also plenty of stories involving water and death. From stories of sirens that would enchant sailors on the open seas, to local legends of old hags that live in ponds waiting to drown those who come too close, the association with death is unavoidable. Again, the water witch does not shy away from death but understands that it is a necessary part of life. It also means that we can use the element of water to help us connect with and send messages to those who have passed on and connect with our ancestors.

Creativity

Creativity is an aspect that I have already mentioned that I ascribe to the element of water despite it being most commonly associated with the element of air. Creativity manifests itself in many different ways. It isn't just painting or poetry – we can add creativity to almost every area of our lives. The element of water encourages us to embrace our creativity, to play and explore. If you are attempting to make a living through your artwork, your writing, your music, etc., then the element of water can help you find success.

Intuitive Practice

Last, but by no means least, the water witch to me is someone who follows their intuition and seeks to become more in tune with it. All things related to the psychic and the subconscious are associated with the element of water. Dreaming, divination, and intuition are all governed by this element. In a sense, this ties in with many of the other attributes. As the water witch seeks knowledge, they will often use their 'psychic gifts' such as divination to gain this insight. When going through a period of transformation or change, we can use meditation, journeying, and working with guides to gain the strength and deeper insight to see through this transformation.

I'm personally not a big fan of the term 'psychic'. It gives the illusion that there is some special gift that is only bestowed upon certain people and that it is something mystical and difficult to obtain. My view on it is the opposite. Anybody can become 'psychic'. Sure, some people have more of a disposition towards these abilities and are more in tune with them, but anybody can learn them. It isn't something 'mystical', but rather something present in all people, and even those who don't believe in the spiritual use such powers unknowingly. It's that gut feeling that tells you to choose a certain book, or to avoid a certain way home. I personally believe that the water witch actively seeks to practice and rely on these abilities to guide them through their everyday life.

The above are just the main aspects of working with the element of water that I feel particularly drawn to. Maybe you want to walk this path in order to help you manage your emotions, or to bring more love and beauty into your life. Or perhaps one of your main interests is dream work and you want to use this element to enhance it. Whatever path you decide to take, walk it with conviction and make it your own.

Chapter 2

Water Through the Ancient World

From the earliest civilizations, water has played a key part in cultural evolution and human survival. By learning the ways of our ancestors, we can tap into ancient knowledge and strengthen our connection with the element of water by increasing our understanding of, and demonstrating our gratitude for this life giving energy. The history of the world is vast, and there is a lot to cover, so I have in no way attempted to give you a comprehensive overview. Instead, I have picked five cultures and civilizations and given a very brief taste as to their relationship with water. I know that some people find this sort of commentary quite dry, and I understand that reading this section doesn't give you anything practical you can go away and try. However, I believe that developing this understanding as to how our ancestors lived and the way that water has shaped the world that we live in is important. This information can also help you when we get to the section on working with water spirits. So, bear with me, and use the below to reflect on just how much this element has shaped our world.

Mesopotamia

The Mesopotamian era is considered to consist of the first civilizations. The developments made during the Mesopotamian era were some of the most important in human history; they invented the wheel, agricultural practices, the written alphabet, mathematics, and astronomy. It included several dominant cultures during its time, the most notable being the Sumerians, the Assyrians, and the Babylonians. They ruled at different points from roughly 4000 BC. The end of the Mesopotamian era is often defined as up until Babylon fell to the Persians in 539 BC.

Mesopotamia was situated within the Tigris – Euphrates river system, in a tract between the two rivers in what is now modern day Iraq. One poem from the Babylonian era, a creation tale called *Enuma Elish* describes how before the heavens and earth there were the ocean waters of Tiamat and the freshwaters of her husband Apsu, and when these two mingled they created the Gods. These Gods went on to create the heavens and earth (following a war between the Gods in which both Tiamat and Apsu were slain).

As well as the rivers themselves, the Mesopotamians relied on canals and wells for their survival. The rivers were prone to flooding, but this was seen as a necessity for the Mesopotamians as it boosted their agricultural efforts. Whilst at first they were dependent on this flooding, their development of agricultural practices meant that they became able to manage their crops without being completely reliant on the floods.

By meditating on the way in which the Mesopotamians used and relied on water and the impact it had on the building of the very first civilisations, we can gain a deep appreciation for this element. It truly is one of the building blocks of life.

It is also a great example of the way in which water ebbs and flows and changes, very much in the same way life does, and how we can adapt to those changes. Like the floods that would wash over the land, sometimes we are powerless against this change. However devastating this change may seem, often it is necessary to make way for new growth. But sometimes we can learn to harness and control this change, and direct it towards a better outcome.

Ancient Egypt

Ancient Egypt experienced an overlap with the peoples of Mesopotamia in regards to timelines. Due to the conditions and the environment they lived in, we can see many similarities in the beliefs and practices between the Egyptians and those civilizations of the Mesopotamian era. This is especially evident when we consider their reliance on the element of water.

The Nile was their main source of water and would also flood yearly. It also played an important part in their beliefs surrounding the afterlife, as they believed that water transported the soul of the dead to the afterlife. Many of the Egyptian dead were buried with small boats in the hopes that they would be transported to the afterlife, equating rivers and water with death and the journey to the afterlife.

There were many different deities associated with water throughout the hundreds of years that the ancient Egyptians reigned. This includes Anuket who was the Goddess of the Nile and would nourish the fields, Hapi who was the God specifically of the annual flooding of the Nile, and Tefnut, the Goddess of water and moisture.

From the Ancient Egyptians we can begin to see how death is connected with the element of water. Drawing from their belief that water would help ferry the dead to the afterlife or the otherworld, we can see how the element of water is often associated with spirit work, divination, and different types of journeying.

Ancient Greeks

There is plenty of evidence for water use throughout Ancient Greece. Practically, they constructed aqueducts, sewer systems, constructed fountains and baths for hygienic purposes, flushing toilets, an indoor plumbing system to utilize pressurized showers, pressurized piping to aid in firefighting, and even created and used one of the first known examples of the waterwheel. It was the Greeks who came up with the four classical elements which we still use today – earth, air, fire, and water.

The Greeks had many different water deities, and like other civilizations also had deities associated with specific rivers, fountains, etc. There were deities of the sea such as Poseidon, but there were also deities that focused on specific aspects of the sea or water. For example, there was Palaemon, a God who helped sailors in distress upon the seas, and the Goddess Cymopoleia who was a daughter of Poseidon and also known as the Goddess of giant storm waves.

The Ancient Greeks also gave us the lost city of Atlantis, possibly the most famous of all the lost civilizations. It was first mentioned by Plato around 360 BC. According to Plato, Atlantis existed roughly 9,000 years before then, and the story had been passed down orally through the ages – up until Plato, there were no written accounts of Atlantis. The inhabitants of Atlantis were half God and half human and the island itself full of moats, waterways, and a large canal that ran through the island. Atlantis was known as a utopia, a place of spiritual and moral goodness. However, its people eventually turned to greed and immorality which angered the Gods. As punishment they sent earthquakes and fire which destroyed the island and caused it to sink.

Whilst many scholars believe that Plato created this story to support his philosophical writings, that hasn't stopped people from searching for this lost civilization. There is evidence of similar events happening throughout history; roughly 3,600 years ago a volcanic eruption destroyed the island of Santorini near Greece. The Island was home to an advanced society of Minoans at the time, but following the eruption the Minoan civilisation all but disappeared. Whether Atlantis existed as a real place or not, its legend has persisted throughout the ages, and some water witches work with Atlantean energies in their practice, some believing that the supernatural race still resides in this city lost beneath the ocean.

Greek mythology also includes the Nymphs. There were many different types of Nymph, including water Nymphs. Nymphs are often referred to as minor nature deities, and were often seen more as a personification of the land around them than distinct and individual beings.

There were two types of Nymph associated with water; the Naiads who were associated with fresh water, and the Nereids who were associated with the sea. There were subsets of Nymph below these two as well. For example, Potameides were Naiads which presided over rivers, and Pegaeae were Naiads which presided over lakes. The Nymphs were described as beautiful and otherworldly, and there are several accounts of Greek Gods and mortals falling in love with Nymphs. However, there was also a dangerous side to them, and they could strike a human dumb or send them into a state of madness. Humans also risked becoming infatuated with these minor deities, obsessively so. We will look at different water spirits and such a bit later in the book, but through the ancient Greeks we start to explore our connection to the element of water through working with various different deities and water spirits.

Ancient Rome

One of the most notable areas of water worship around the Roman period was through their use of baths. Roman baths often seemed to be places of worship, with one of the most famous being the Roman baths in the town of Bath in the UK. When the Romans conquered Britain in 43 CE, they constructed this temple and bath in honour of the deity Sulis Minerva, who is believed to be a blending of the Celtic Goddess Sulis and the Roman Goddess Minerva. It soon became one of the most important pilgrimage sites associated with the Western Roman Empire.

Several curse tablets have also been found at this spring, although this was not a practice which was specific to the Romans – curse tablets and similar have also been found in Greek sites and Egyptian sites. Curses would be written on lead or pewter and then thrown into the spring, where the Goddess would heed their request. Roughly 130 of these tablets have been found at the spring in Bath, and interestingly all but one of them concerned the return of stolen goods to its rightful owner. The 'curse' was not a curse in the sense of wishing harm on another; rather, it was asking Sulis to exact a punishment of her choosing on the thief if the goods were not returned.

The Romans also honoured Genii, or Genius. This was a belief that everyone and everything contained a divine spirit that watched over that particular person or location. Lares were a type of Genius and although often described as household Gods, they also watched over towns, cities, bodies of water, livestock, and more.

I find the ritualistic importance of the Roman baths fascinating. It begins to demonstrate how the element of water can be used in rituals and rites to honour ourselves and our deities, and be used to help us manifest our desires. There is also an interesting balance between how baths and springs were used to celebrate and petition deities for good fortune, but also to curse or threaten. Here we can see an understanding of the nature of deities and the element of water. What is often considered to be the 'dark' side of spirits and deities is acknowledged and worked with as well as the 'light', and provides an interesting insight into the dual nature of those associated with the element of water.

Ancient Celts

The Ancient Celts are not just one 'people', but several. At one point, they were the largest group of people to inhabit ancient Europe, and are generally identified through their use of language and other cultural similarities. There were many different groups that made up what we refer to as 'the Celtic peoples', and these different groups had different practices, deities, spirits, etc. It is easy to lump them all under the term Celtic, but it is really important to notice and respect the differences between the cultures that are included within the term Celtic.

The Celts had many local deities, and specific rivers, springs, and areas of natural significance often had a very specific deity associated with them. Deities who were the personification of specific rivers were also present.

As well as deities associated with types of water and specific bodies of water, there were also the fae. I use the term 'fae' loosely as a bit of a catch-all. For example, in the Irish tradition they are often known as the Aos Sí and in Welsh the Tylwyth Teg.

Whilst there are variations between different traditions, generally these were otherworldly beings, and some were said to inhabit or personify bodies of water. They feature in myths and tales throughout the Celtic period. One of my personal favourite figures is The Lady of the Lake from Welsh Arthurian legend. There are several stories which involve a Lady of the Lake, such as she who gave King Arthur the sword Excalibur, or who raised the knight Lancelot. However, there is some debate as to whether all these tales were about the one being or whether there were multiple ladies of the lake.

Welsh mythology also has its own lost civilization, that of Avalon. Many believe that Avalon was a real, physical place, with the most popular potential location being that of Glastonbury in the UK (which at the time could have been surrounded by marshland and so could have been considered an 'island' of sorts). Avalon first appeared around 1150 AC in a piece of work called *Vita Merlini* written by Geoffrey of Monmouth, where the wounded King Arthur is brought to receive healing from Morgen. Avalon itself is said to be a land of plenty; where apples and grains grow unaided and nine sisters – including Morgen – rule by a 'pleasing' set of laws.

One of the most prominent aspects of Celtic water worship was how they revered springs, fountains, wells, etc. They were said to bring healing, as well as provide a bridge between our world and the other. As I've mentioned in the previous chapter, healing is one of the aspects of water witchcraft that is very important to me, and so the Celts connection between the element of water and healing fascinates me. The Celts honoured nature, and through them we can see how a connection to the natural waters around us can lead to profound spiritual growth and healing.

Chapter 3

Connecting with Water Energies

As you may have guessed, a connection with the element of water is crucial to the water witch. Not only do you need to 'find' this connection, but maintain it too. For some people this comes instinctively. However, for many it doesn't, and even if you are one of those who have a natural affinity for this element you can still work on strengthening it. If you are new to water witchcraft or are just here because you want to improve your connection with the element of water as opposed to making it the main focus of your practice then I recommend you start small. Even the tiniest of interactions with this element can have a profound effect. In my experience, little and often is the best approach. A quick activity or small gesture performed once or twice a day will most likely aid you much more than a large ritual performed just once a week.

One of the best things you can do which will enhance your ability to work with the water element is to connect with bodies of water around you. Each body of water is different; it moves and flows with its own energy. Think of it as a living, breathing being. I have several ponds within walking distance which I have built a connection with, and it is one of the most rewarding elements of my practice. I have been to visit them almost every day since I moved here, and each one brings me something different.

Go for a walk and see if there are any particular ponds, rivers, brooks, etc., nearby that you could connect with. Visit them as often as you can, make offerings, thank them, and welcome their energy into your life. Don't be afraid to talk to them as if they were your friends – tell them your hopes, your fears, any frustrations you have or joyous news. Make sure you listen to them too – open your heart and show gratitude for any messages the water may have for you.

One of the things I hear most often from the new witches that I mentor is that they don't feel like they can call themselves witches because they just don't have time to practice. I remember feeling like that when I first started out too. We talk about witchcraft being a lifestyle but you can't just click your fingers and expect your life to change overnight. You need to build new habits and you need to consciously practice those habits until they stick. This can be some effort to begin with, but it is absolutely worth it. Don't be disheartened if you can't stick to it or don't feel it right away. As with all things, this can take practice. Sometimes we have shut ourselves off for so long that it can take a while to open ourselves up to these energies. So even if it doesn't work with the first meditation or the first blessing, keep at it. Try different approaches, search for more ideas than just what is in this book, and keep at it until you find something that works for you. It is difficult to put into words exactly what this connection feels like as everyone experiences it differently, but you will know it when you feel it.

Below I have included some ideas as to ways you can connect with this element in your day-to-day routine. You don't need to perform elaborate rituals, or run naked through a stream to achieve this (although if that's how you best connect to water energies, then go for it!). By incorporating small and regular activities into our practice, we can start to build a lifestyle which is truly magical and will serve us moving forward.

Water Energy Meditation

This is great meditation for when you need a bit of an energy boost. I personally enjoy performing it in the mornings to get me ready for the day ahead. It brings a subtle energy that washes through us, awakening each of our chakras and bringing us the peace and balance we need. This meditation can be as long or short as you want – even five minutes can make a difference.

First, prepare and enter a meditative state in whatever manner you usually do. I personally sit cross legged on the sofa (to make sure there is something there to support my back). In this meditation, we will be visualizing a wave of water travelling up from our root chakra, through our other chakras, and up to our crown chakra. Then we visualize it flowing back down again, back through the chakras, back to the root chakra.

Energy flows through the body aren't quite that straight forward, but for the purposes of this meditation, we will be working with a very simple 'up and down' flow. Trust that doing this will help activate the other energy flows in the body, giving you that boost that you need.

Focus on regulating your breathing; you need to keep it slow, but consistent. Breathe in for a count of three, four, or maybe even five, and then breathe out for the same count. If you find that you are breathing too slowly or too quickly as you progress through the meditation, then feel free to change the count, but try to find one you can stick with for the entirety of the meditation.

Try to connect with the energy of water. If you have worked with water energies before then this may come easily to you. If you haven't then focus on holding the image of water in your mind. It could be the sea, a lake, or even the rain falling and bouncing off the ground. Whatever you decide to use, hold this image for a couple of minutes and tell yourself that you are connecting to the energies of water.

Continue by feeling, or visualizing, a small wave sitting just below your root chakra. Just focus on this first; see it sloshing around gently, like a tiny wave in the sea. Maybe you can even hear it, as if you were standing on a beach and listening to the waves travel up the shoreline. Know that as it moves around your body it will balance and energize you.

When you feel ready, inhale; and as you do, see this wave of energy rising up the left hand side of your body. See it passing through your root chakra, then your sacral, solar plexus, heart, throat, third eye, and finishing at the top of your crown chakra. As it moves through every chakra it empowers that chakra, making it glow brighter.

As you finish inhaling, the wave should have travelled up the length of your body and to the crown chakra. Now, exhale, and see this wave flowing down the right side of your body; back through the crown chakra, the third eye, throat, heart, solar plexus, sacral, and finally finishing at the bottom of the root chakra. Again, see this energy empowering and invigorating each chakra as it passes through. Then, inhale again, and keep this wave of energy flowing, up through the chakras on the left hand side, and down through the chakras on the right hand side. Try to time this perfectly with your breath, so that you aren't holding your breath at either the root or crown chakra, or having to speed up your breathing to catch up with your visualization.

Perform this for several rounds, and when you feel you have finished, come out of meditation as you usually would. You can use this meditation as an energetic pick-me-up, to connect with the energies of water, or you could keep a specific intent in mind and direct the energy towards manifesting that intent.

Daily Blessings

A daily blessing is a great way to just take a moment out to help you connect with water energies. These can be as simple or elaborate as you like and as quick or as long as you would like. Ideas for simple blessings include:

- Wash your hands, whilst focusing on connecting with the water. How does it make you feel? Are there any specific qualities you wish to draw from the water today – maybe to cleanse, or to bring emotional balance? You may also wish to say a little chant, to acknowledge this connection you have with the water.

- Keep a bowl of water on your altar, and use it to anoint yourself. You can use regular tap water, or you might want to use moon water, rain water, or water steeped with specific herbs or crystals. You can use this to anoint your third eye or over your heart chakra – wherever you feel most comfortable. Again, you may wish to say a little prayer to affirm this connection.
- Make an offering of water; this could even be as simple as watering your plants. Remember that water gives life, and how important it is to all plants and creatures to sustain ourselves as you do so.
- Saying a prayer or a poem will also do; it is great if you can include physical water into your blessing, but sometimes a few words of acknowledgement and gratitude will do.

Mantras

Mantras are a quick and simple way of helping you connect with the energy of water. Below are some of my go-to mantras which you may want to try out, or come up with your own. As you do so, visualize the sea, a flowing river, or calming pond, and mentally connect with it as you repeat your mantra:

I am of water, and water connects us all. From the land to the sea, we are one

Rain falls, rivers flow, waves rise and fall; I move with the tides, at one with the power of water

Peace be upon me, peace be within me; I align myself with the element of water, and bring stillness and balance into my life

Energy of water flow through me; guide me and empower me. I am at one with the element of water.

Charms, Trinkets, and Color Magic

Wearing, or keeping with you charms and trinkets which remind you of the element of water, or perhaps a particular body of water you connect to, can help. I personally love the sea. I have a cockle shell with a natural hole in that I found on the beach which I wear as a necklace. I also have a mini mandala made up of shells and crystals on my desk as I work from home and spend most time there, and a small vial of water I collected from Glastonbury's Chalice Wells on a keyring. Even my phone background is a picture of the sea. From shell-based decorations, to artwork, there are many ways you can decorate your space or yourself to keep the energy of water with you. Colors associated with water are blues and greens, and even wearing a scarf of that colour can help you build this connection.

Take a Bath or Shower

Most of us tend to take a bath of shower daily, and usually this is quite a practical activity. We hop in, have a wash, and hop out. However, taking even just an extra minute to actually connect with the energies of water can make a difference. Ritual baths, showers, using specific soaps and scrubs can help to bring additional magic into your routine. Later on we will look in more detail at ritual baths and showers, but for now try to take that little bit of time when you bathe/shower to connect with the water around you.

Exercises

Choose at least three of the above exercises and try to perform one each day for at least five days. Before you start, make a note in your journal as to how you currently feel your connection with the element of water stands. Are you one of those people who has a natural disposition towards this element, or maybe you are here because you don't feel a connection with it at all and want to change that? Do you have any expectations as to how this connection will feel or how it may affect you?

After performing one of these exercises every day, make sure you write your experience down in your journal straight away.

Even if it didn't work, write it all down – what you tried, how you felt, if there was anything you could feel that was holding you back or causing a distraction, etc.

Finally, at the end of the five days, write about how you feel now and your overall experience. Has anything changed? Were there any notable experiences or any particular exercises which worked well for you?

Once the five days are up, don't stop there! Make sure you perform these exercises regularly. I would say that once a day is ideal, but I also appreciate that sometimes life can make it difficult to practice every day.

Chapter 4

Tools of the Water Witch

The water witch tends to use tools as any other witch would. However, often these can be 'water themed' to help us connect with water energies – for example, using a wand made out of driftwood or a piece of tree fished out of a pond or river. Whilst there isn't actually much that a water witch uses that you wouldn't find in other practices, they might perhaps use some tools more so than you would find in other practices. Below I will take you through some of the most common ones, and how they are used.

Driftwood: As I mentioned above, driftwood can be used to make wands. It can also be used to create divination tools, charms, or sigils, and is great to carve symbols into. Basically, anything a stick can be used for, driftwood can be used for.

Bottles of Water: A water witch collects different types of water, and each body of water has its own association (more on that later in the book). Try to use glass bottles as opposed to plastic water bottles. Not only are plastic bottles terrible for the environment, but over time the plastic from these bottles can leach into the water. But trust me when I say that you will never have enough bottles, so start building your collection now!

Hag Stones: Hag stones are stones with natural holes in, and are most often found on the beach or near large bodies of water. They have a rich history in folklore and tradition, but most commonly hag stones can be used to bring luck and protection. They are often worn as charms or used in magic. I have a large hag stone I found on the beach which I anointed with protection oil, and now sits by my front door to protect my home.

Sea Glass: Again, often found on the beach, it is formed when pieces of glass are smoothed by the salt in the sea. Sea glass can be of any color, and these are useful to use as color magic correspondences, to draw symbols and sigils on for charms and divination tools, or to decorate an altar. I also find that they make good offerings for sea deities, and pieces of sea glass are a glorious find.

Sand: Collected from the beach where it has been exposed to the water, most sand contains tiny little particles of minerals such as quartz, garnet, black tourmaline, and beryl (amongst others). The breaking down of these minerals and other things which eventually form sand is not a quick process – some sands are as old as 4 billion years! As such, sand can be used to represent the cycles of life, transformation, and anything to do with the past such as ancestor, or past life work. The sands also act as a barrier between the land and the sea, and as such can be seen as a barrier between worlds.

Mermaids Purses: Mermaids purses are the egg sacs of certain sea creatures such as the skate. They are black/brown rectangular 'pods', with a tendril at each of the four corners. These are very much like 'chicken eggs' to the water witch, and can be used in magic around fertility. As the word 'purse' may indicate, they are also associated with abundance and money magic.

Bones and Animal Parts: Working with animal parts is not something that everyone feels comfortable with, no matter their path. You don't have to work with them if you don't want to, it is a personal preference. However, bones and other animal parts, such as a crab claws, can be used in magic. They are mostly used to help connect with the spirit of that particular animal to bring guidance, or in magic based around the associations of that animal. For example, one of the attributes of the lobster is independence, so you could use a lobster claw in workings to bring you independence. The shark is associated with action, so you might wear a shark tooth necklace when you need help with motivation.

Salt: Salt is often associated with the element of earth, but it is also associated with water, especially the sea – the sea is salt water after all. Salt is a strong protector and purifier, and is often used to protect our personal space and to cleanse objects.

Crystals: Whilst crystals are most often associated with the element of earth, there are some which are also associated with the element of water. These are mostly blue colored crystals, such as turquoise and aquamarine. Some green crystals, such as green aventurine (as well as blue aventurine) are also used to help connect with sea energies.

Herbs/Plants/Trees: Again, herbs are most often associated with the element of earth. However, they can be combined with water (in teas, ritual baths, etc.), to help boost your magic. There are also some which are more strongly associated with the element of water. Bladderwrack, or seaweed, is an obvious example. There are also a lot of plants which are found close to bodies of water which can be used to connect with water energies, and some more general in which their innate properties make them more connected with the element of water than any other element.

Plants

Bladderwrack: Bladderwrack is a type of seaweed. It can be used to protect those who are sailing or flying over the sea. It is also associated with the moon and lunar energies, and despite its appearance can also be used in beauty magic.

Bladderwrack is also said to aid in weather magic. One can conjure a storm by waving it in a circular motion above their heads. It can also be hung outside of the house to help predict the weather. If the weather will be warm and dry then the bladderwrack will stay dry and crisp. However, if rain is on the horizon, then the bladder wrack will turn moist.

Other uses for bladderwrack include in abundance magic, and spells concerning business, financial security, helping to remove negativity, and to aid in otherworld travel.

Lotus Flower: The lotus flower's roots are submerged in the mud and during the night the flower submerges down into the water. The next morning it will bloom back above the water, and then disappear back down at nightfall. As such, it is often associated with life, growth, and rebirth, especially in a spiritual sense. The Egyptians believed that the lotus had the power to bring the dead back to life in the form of a lotus flower themselves, and in Hindu tradition it is said that the Gods sit on lotus thrones.

The individual colors of the lotus also carry specific meanings. For example, the yellow lotus is associated with spiritual ascension and religious belief, and the white lotus is associated with purity, balance, faith, beauty, wealth, knowledge, and fertility.

Reeds: The reed is one of the plants/trees associated with the Irish Tree Ogham. It has had many practical uses, such as being used as flooring or roofing. You can soak them in fat to create candles, and it is still used today to make instruments. Reeds can be used for purification and protection, and to rid yourself or your space of negative energies. It is also associated with being proactive and helping you find your purpose.

Water Lily: The water lily represents femininity, beauty, innocence and purity. It functions in a similar way to the lotus flower; lilies will submerge themselves in the water and turn into a fruit. It will then return to the surface and spread its seeds across the water. As such it is also associated with transformation, rebirth, and improving oneself. Another function that the water lily performs is to act as a filter and purify the water around it. As such, it can also be used to remove negativity.

Cattails: Cattails are a type of reed with a rich history in folklore, and have been used for almost any purpose you can think of. According to Scott Cunningham, it has a masculine energy and is associated with fire. However, I think this plant has a fairly balanced energy between the masculine and feminine. Not only can it be used for strength and lust, but also to bring peace, especially between two people. Like other water plants, it has the ability to detoxify water and remove pollutants. This makes this plant great at absorbing negativity. However, it cannot get rid of these harmful toxins straight away, so make sure you dispose of it once it has done its job.

Other herbs/plants/scents associated with the element of water include spearmint, lemon verbena, the ash tree, the birch tree, water fern, lavender, apple, coconut, daffodils, eucalyptus, hyacinth (especially water hyacinth), rose, the willow tree, thyme, lilies in general, and ylang-ylang.

Seashells

Of course, we can't write a whole book about water magic and not include a section on seashells. There are many different types of seashells, and many have different properties. Think of them as the crystals of the sea in a sense, for they can be used in the same way. As you might carry around a piece of citrine in your purse to ensure wealth and abundance, you might instead carry a small cowrie shell. One of my favourite ways to use seashells is in 'crystal grids', but replacing crystals with shells. I use these mainly for healing purposes and find them to be extremely effective. For example, a grid consisting of a starfish, clams, cockles, limpet shells, whelk shells, and clear quartz crystals is great for bringing relief and renewal after a period of difficulty.

Below is a look at some of the more common types of shell and their associations. If you head to the beach to collect shells, make sure you leave enough for the local wildlife – many small creatures use shells as their home. Make sure to also check restrictions in your area, as some places prohibit the removal of shells and such from their beaches.

Some shells can be difficult to tell apart. The conch shell and the whelk shell are two which are often confused, so make sure you do your research. Take into account your location and the environment around you; for example, conchs are generally found in tropical waters whilst whelks are found in more temperate waters. Sometimes this might be the only way in which you can identify that shell you found, so pay attention.

I also recommend working with any shells you find and learning what their associations mean to you. When I first started out, I read that the ark shell was great for inner reflection. So, after a particularly bad day at work I did a smoke cleanse on myself using some 'ocean wind' incense, and then sat down to meditate with an ark shell. I wanted to reflect on the day, what had gone wrong, and what I could do in the future to ensure it didn't happen again. However, the ark shell had very different ideas. I felt a very masculine energy from it, and it was one of acceptance and moving on rather than reflecting. It told me that what was done was done; there was no point in dwelling on it, tomorrow was a new day, and I had the strength to ensure that I didn't let one bad day get me down. This was quite a surprise considering everything I had read about the ark shell. So, don't take what I have written here as gospel. You may find the shells speak to you differently.

Abalone: Commonly used as a smudging bowl for those who practice smudging, it is also associated with healing, prosperity, and abundance.

Ark: The ark shell has quite a masculine energy, and can help us feel stable and secure. It allows us to put the past behind us and move forward with strength and determination.

Auger: The auger shell promotes focus and clarity, as well as protection.

Carrier: Carrier shells are fascinating. Often the creature inhabiting this shell will cement other shells and small stones to the edge of this shell as it grows, and there are some beautiful ones out there. As such, the carrier shell is associated with abundance, growth, development, and creativity. It can be useful to those who wish to come 'out of their shell' or explore their own personality, individuality, or creative expression.

Clam: The clam has many different associations; these include communication, grounding, healing, love, purification, emotional protection, and helping us connect with the world around us.

Cockle: Associated with love, joy, contentment, and new beginnings. It is a great shell to use for emotional balance.

Conch: The conch shell has a very feminine energy. It can be used to promote love and beauty, as well as knowledge, wisdom, and magic.

Cowry: The cowry shell is most often associated with abundance, prosperity, and wealth. It can also be used to increase fertility and encourage personal growth.

Limpet: The limpet brings us the confidence and courage needed to endure difficult situations, or those where we may feel unsure of ourselves. It teaches tenacity, of 'clinging on' and persevering. It can also bring wisdom, and help us to realize when it may in fact be time to let go rather than clinging on to that which no longer serves us.

Mussel: The mussel shell has quite a gentle energy. It can help us to feel more connected in our relationships and with those around us. I find that this shell gives off strong lunar vibes with the colouring of the inside of the shell. It can also help bring us peace and a sense of stability when going through difficult periods.

Periwinkle: The periwinkle is associated with friendships and platonic relationships. It can also bring grounding and help us stay focused.

Sand Dollar: The sand dollar shell is in fact an endoskeleton of a sand dollar, which is a type of burrowing sea urchin. With its flower-like imprint, the sand dollar represents balance, harmony, and completeness. It is also associated with transformation, wisdom, and opening ourselves up to the secrets of the world around us.

Scallop: The scallop is another shell associated with Goddess energies. It can bring healing, and lift our spirits. It brings love, beauty, relaxation and regeneration. It can also be used to encourage change, and help us navigate change with a positive attitude.

Starfish: The starfish is often seen as a sign of fortune and used as a good luck charm. It also represents renewal, and is good for those who are recovering from a period of negativity.

Slipper: I find that the slipper shell has quite a feminine energy. It represents balance and encourages compassion and selflessness.

Whelk: The whelk is one of my favourite shells. It represents knowledge, wisdom, and imagination, and can help us when we need guidance or inspiration. I have heard whelks referred to as 'the bullies of the sea' in the wild, and so can also be used for strength or to help you overcome adversity.

The Water Witches Altar/Shrine

I'll preface this by saying, you don't need an altar. It isn't a requirement. For years I didn't have a permanent altar or shrine set up. I moved around a lot, often living in pretty bad rented accommodation and with people I didn't know too well, so my 'house' was pretty much just somewhere to sleep. I much preferred to be out in the forest or parks and working magic discreetly. Now I am fortunate enough to be in a position where I have my own space and feel comfortable having one displayed. However, if you live in shared accommodation without much privacy, or are trying to be more low-key in your practices for whatever reason, then don't feel like you need to have one prominently displayed. If you do want an altar or shrine, even just a small lay out on the edge of a desk can work. One of the great things about water witchcraft is that many of the tools we work with can be seen as nice little decorative pieces; statues depicting mermaids, seafolk, and other mythical creatures, shells, bottles of sand, etc.

Whether you want to go all out for your altar or shrine or go for something a bit more discreet, what you display on your altar is completely up to you. Every witch's set-up is different, and should represent them and their beliefs. The water witch is no different.

There is a subtle difference between an altar and a shrine. An altar is generally a place where practical workings take place; it holds your tools and other more general magical items (such as representations of the elements, spell jars, herbs, crystals, etc.) and many witches perform their rituals and spells at their altar. A shrine is usually dedicated to a specific deity, spirit, your ancestors, etc. It acts as a space of worship, containing statues, offerings, and anything that reminds you of that which you have dedicated it to.

Personally, my set-up is a shrine rather than an altar. I have a small space which I have dedicated to the Goddess and water spirits I work with and water energies in general. It is filled with statues and charms representing my deity and animal guide, shells, my offering bowl, and other bits and pieces which I think they would enjoy to help strengthen my connection to them. I do all of my magical workings in a separate space as it just feels more appropriate (and despite having my own space, it isn't a lot of space). I like to think of my shrine as something ever changing, that grows with me. I visit it at least once a day just to say thanks and show gratitude for the guidance I am given and the blessings in my life, even if it is just a quick 'thank you'. I try to tend to my shrine every couple of weeks; this could mean cleansing it with salt water and incense smoke and reiterating that it is a shrine dedicated to my Goddess, water spirits, and the element of water, or adding/removing items when it feels right. Whether you decide to work with an altar or a shrine, this is a sacred place and should be treated as such.

Below are some items you might find on the water witches' altar or shrine. Of course, add whatever feels right to you, but the below might provide you with some ideas to get started with.

- Statues or charms that represent your deity, your guides, or the element of water in general.
- Artwork which reminds you of your connection with water; this could, for example, be a photo that you have taken, a picture of the sea or the rain you found online, or a postcard from a sacred well you visited.
- A small bowl to make offerings in.

- Blue crystals to represent water.
- Shells, pebbles collected from the beach, sea glass, and hag stones.
- A small bottle of salt.
- A small bottle of sand.
- Bottles of different types of water, such as sun water, rain water, moon water, or maybe some sprays you have made (such as a 'success spray', the recipe for which you can find in the 'spells' section).
- A cloth to decorate the space with and protect the surface of whatever you are using; colours such as blue, green, or white work well for the water witch.

Exercises

As you can see, there are many different tools that the water witch could use in their practice. Have a think about the tools you already use in your practice and whether you could incorporate more water inspired versions. For example, if you read runes, could you collect some light coloured shells or pebbles from the beach and draw your runes onto them? If you enjoy working with color magic, could you incorporate different colored sea glass into your practice? Even small things, such as swapping out your shower gel for one with a scent more closely associated with water such as coconut, or a soap which contains seaweed, can boost your connection to water energies.

Have a think about whether you do want any sort of dedicated space, and if you do, will it be an altar or a shrine? Once you have made this decision, take your time and design your own altar or shrine. If a shrine, is there a particular deity or spirit you want to dedicate it to, or maybe you just want to dedicate it to water energies in general?

Decide what you want on your altar or shrine. You might want to sketch out a rough idea of how you want it to look, or you might just want to dive straight into it and let your intuition guide you in regards to what to include and how to display it. This space should be a reflection of your inner witch, a sacred place, so treat it with love and respect.

Chapter 5

Water Deities

With the importance of water being recognized in practically every civilization since the beginning of recorded time, there are a wealth of different Gods and Goddesses you can work with if you choose to do so. This means that it doesn't matter which pantheon you prefer to work with or what path you follow, for chances are you will be able to find a water deity that calls to you.

I personally have found water deities to be among some of the most friendly and helpful that I have worked with. However, in many tales and depictions, deities are akin to humans in the sense that they are not completely 'good' or 'evil'. Like us, deities also have their flaws and what you might refer to as their dark side. Some of these tales involve some pretty nasty behaviour, so always make sure to do your research before working with a deity.

Why work with a water deity? Deities can act as guides and mentors, to help push us to be the best that we can be. They can inspire us, protect us, and aid us in manifesting our desires into the world. Unsurprisingly, working with water deities can help strengthen our connection to the element of water and further empower us. The notion of the elements or the divine is somewhat abstract, and one of the reasons that deities from many cultures have been depicted as being humanlike is that it makes it easier to connect with them. In the same way, working with a deity when practicing water magic can help us better harness and connect with the energies of the water element.

One statement I hear a lot when it comes to working with deities is that you need to wait for a God or Goddess to choose you. I personally don't subscribe to this notion. If a deity is trying to get your attention, then great! But if not, don't let that stop you from searching for one and approaching them to see if they would be willing to let you work with them.

If you are searching for a God or Goddess to work with, first off think about which pantheon you feel most comfortable with. Then, start researching. Despite all having water in common with each other, many deities have different attributes and associations. Think about what it is that you are looking for in a deity, as if you were writing a 'wish list' of things you want to find in a mentor. Are you particularly interested in the otherworld, healing, creativity, etc.? Are you looking for a deity who is known to be friendly, or would you prefer a blunter approach? Research authors or practitioners who have worked with any deity you are interested in, native historical resources, books, museum guides, and anywhere else you can find information. Any information you find can help you determine if the God or Goddess you have chosen is indeed right for you.

Research is all well and good, but once you have identified the one you want to try and work with, you then need to put the effort in to build a relationship with them. Working with deities is a two way street and working with water deities is no different. You will only get out what you put into it. There are many different ways you can honour your chosen God or Goddess – below are just a few ideas. Remember, the connection you have with your deity is unique, and you should listen to what your deity desires. For example, I have a specific incense that I found, the scent of which my Goddess absolutely loves; I can feel their presence much more strongly once I light this incense. Experiment, within reason, to find out what works for you, and always remember to treat your deity with respect and gratitude. Throwing a tantrum and demanding things of your deity is not likely to put you in their good books.

- A statue or other representation of them on your altar or elsewhere in your house.
- Build a small shrine to them.
- Go for a walk next to water and try to feel the presence of your deity; some deities are associated with particular bodies of water or features of water, such as the sea or wells.
- Write a poem or song for your deity, or dedicate a piece of artwork for them.
- Create a herbal mixture to use as an offering.
- Bless water in their name and use it to anoint yourself during your daily blessings or when performing your mantras.
- Dedicate a piece of jewellery to them and wear it when you want to strengthen your connection.
- Just talk to them! Thank them for what they have blessed you with, tell them your hopes and your fears, and listen to what they have to say.

Sometimes, you may go through all of these steps and feel nothing. As I've said with all things, if that's the case then it is OK. It just means that that particular deity connection wasn't meant for you. Pick yourself up, and try again with a different deity. Make sure you put your intention out into the universe, and let it know you are searching for a guide. This can be as simple as saying a quick prayer asking for a deity to guide you. Your prayers may be answered. Signs that a deity may be willing to work with you include seeing animals or symbols associated with a particular deity where you may not usually see them, an instance of that deity appearing in books or articles unexpectedly, images in dreams or during meditation, or sometimes even just a feeling or inkling. Always trust your intuition, and keep your heart open.

If you don't feel comfortable working with a deity, then you don't need to. You can work directly with the energy and the spirits of water instead if that is what you prefer.

Below is a really brief overview of some of the most popular and well-known water deities. With such a wealth of information out there, make sure you research books, videos, online articles, and other means of information to make sure you know exactly what you are getting yourself into when it comes to working with a specific deity. If you don't find one here that calls to you then take your search outside of this book. There are far more water deities than I can write about here, so have fun researching.

Amphitrite: In Greek mythology, Amphitrite was the consort of the sea God Poseidon, and a sea Goddess herself. She is sometimes known as the personification of the sea itself, and was said to give birth to seals, dolphins, and fearsome sea creatures, alongside her more 'human' appearing children. Originally a sea Nymph, she was the eldest of fifty daughters born to Nereus and Doris. Depictions of her usually show her holding one arm up and pinching her fingers together, or surrounded by fish and other sea creatures.

Clíodhna: Clíodhna is considered a member of the Irish Tuatha Dé Danann. In some tales she was the daughter of Manannán mac Lir's Druid who resided with them in The Land of Promise. She was prone to walking the mortal world, and was said to be the most beautiful woman in the earthly world when she did. Eventually she fell in love with a mortal man and left The Land of Promise to be with him permanently. However, displeased with her leaving, she is taken by a wave caused by the music of a minstrel of Manannán mac Lir. In some tales the wave brings her back to The Land of Promise where she remains forevermore, and in some tales, she is drowned.

There are other mentions of Clíodhna in Irish mythology. At some point, she became the Queen of the Banshees and is associated with several old Irish family names. I have worked with Clíodhna in her form as the daughter of Manannán mac Lir's Druid, who dwells in The Land of Promise with her three birds of healing. She is a Goddess of the seashore and of prophecy, the otherworld, and creativity.

Coventina: Coventina was a Romano-British Goddess of wells and springs. There are several references to her, including near the Carrawburgh spring along Hadrian's wall (although the well is supposed to be older than the wall itself). Votive candles and other dedications were found in a walled area of the spring, which is now referred to as Coventina's spring, along with two dedication slabs and ten altars to Coventina and Minerva.

The main attributes associated with Coventina are abundance, prophecy, the cycles of life, birth, and renewal, and purification. Some associate her with healing, and whilst there is little historical evidence for this connection, wells and springs were often revered for their healing powers.

Manannán mac Lir: An Irish God of the sea, he was a member of the Irish Tuatha Dé Danann. He is also seen as the ruler of the otherworld, and the over king of the Tuatha Dé Danann after humans came to populate Ireland. It is said that he uses a thick mist, often referred to as his cloak of invisibility, to hide his home and that of the other remaining Tuatha Dé Danann from mortal eyes.

There are many, many tales which include Manannán mac Lir. Many of these tales involve him giving or receiving magical gifts. He owned a self-navigating boat, a horse which could ride over the sea as well as land, a goblet of truth, and a sword from which any wound was fatal. He certainly has a very jovial presence, and I have always found him to give off a sort of 'father figure' presence whenever I have worked with him.

Nantosuelta: Considered a Celtic deity, evidence of her worship has been found in several locations in France. I worked with Nantosuelta for several years as she embodies the elements of earth and fire as well as the element of water. Rivers are associated with her, as is abundance and the hearth.

Neptune: One of the most well-known Roman deities, Neptune was the God and King of the sea. There is evidence to show that Neptune was actually associated with fresh water springs before he became known as the God of the seas. He is often depicted as an old man with long hair and a grey beard, carrying his infamous trident. He is sometimes depicted as riding a chariot pulled by dolphins.

Neptune was also known for his temper, and there are many stories of him acting out of anger, such as flooding the lands when he lost a contest to Minerva. As well as the seas, he was also said to be associated with storms and the weather, and horses, especially horse racing. He is also associated with fertility, and took many mortal lovers.

The festival of Neptunalia was held on July 23rd, and it was believed that he was called upon to help avoid drought during the summer period.

Palaemon: Another Greek deity. Originally known as Melicertes, his name was later changed to Palaemon when he became a marine deity. It is said that his mother Ino was the one who had raised the infant Dionysus. Consumed by jealousy, Hera drove Ino's husband to insanity, resulting in him 'pursuing' Ino and Melicertes. Ino threw herself and Melicertes from a high rock, and both were turned into deities. Melicertes' body was carried to the Isthmus of Corinth by a dolphin, and left under a pine tree where his uncle Sisyphus found it.

Palaemon is known as a God who protects and aids sailors when in distress. Sharks are also associated with Palaemon.

Poseidon: The Greek God of the sea, similar to Neptune in Roman mythology. He was also the God of horses, earthquakes, droughts and floods. One of the twelve Olympians, he was also considered a chief God of several Greek cities and was also one of the original guardians of the Oracle at Delphi. Sailors would pray to him for a calm crossing as he was seen as a protector and has been described as 'a saviour of ships'.

However, there is also a negative side to Poseidon. He was known for taking many lovers, several of them against their will. It was also said that when he was offended or ignored, he would strike the ground with his trident to create earthquakes and cause ships to sink and men to drown.

Exercises

Think about if you want to work with a deity or not. Remember, you don't have to work with a deity if you don't want to, it isn't a requirement. You may prefer to work directly with the energy of water more generally, or a specific body of water, or water spirits. If you do decide to work with a deity, then have a think about the qualities you would like a deity to have. Is there a particular type of body of water, such as a river, or the sea, that you feel most drawn to? Are you looking for a maternal figure, a jovial figure, a no-nonsense sort of figure? Do you have any particular passions or interests that you might want a deity to guide you in, or any qualities that you would like them to bestow such as protection or wisdom?

Take your journal and write a paragraph on what your ideal deity would look like. Once you have all this, start your research, and see if you can find a deity which fulfils your needs. Most importantly, you should feel drawn to this deity. You may start researching one deity and come across a different one which draws your interest. Trust your intuition and see what your research brings.

Once you have chosen your deity, make an offering to them

and ask them if they are willing to let you work with them. They may have specific colors, animals, symbols, etc., associated with them which you can use for inspiration. If not, then again listen to your intuition. You can make this offering on your altar, or near a body of water if you have access to one. Hopefully your chosen deity will listen, and you will know when they do and accept you. If after making this offering a few times you still don't feel any sort of connection, then it may be worth looking for a different deity.

Chapter 6

Water in Magic

Everything I have written in this book can be used in water magic. Shells can be used in place of crystals, deities can be called upon to help you manifest your intent, and offerings can be left and an altar or shrine to help bring you what you need to succeed. However, there are also some elements of water magic that weren't quite suitable for their own chapters, but also don't really fit elsewhere in this book. So, in this chapter I want to take a look at some of the more 'practical' applications of water in magic, and how you can use them.

Different Types of Water and Their Uses

There are many different types of bodies of water, and each one has a slightly different association. These are great to be incorporated into your practices. Below I have provided an overview of what each represents, and how they can be used.

There is no limit to how you can incorporate different types of water into your practice. Herbal water (aka tea) or crystal water can be prepared and drunk throughout the day, rain water can be used to water your plants, and sea water could be used to wipe down your desk after a particularly hard day to help get rid of any negative energies. Or you may wish to keep a small bowl of snow water on your desk to help bring balance and peace, especially if your job is quite stressful.

I would recommend that you don't ingest any of the below. There is always the chance that water taken from anywhere other than the tap or a bottle contains something nasty in it, and you don't want to make yourself ill. Some wells and other bodies of water are safe for consumption, and often this will be made clear to you via official signs or communications. If in doubt, ask.

Rain Water

Possibly the most often used as it is so accessible. Simply set up a bowl or jar outside, and catch the rain as it falls. Rain water is a great all-purpose water, and often the conditions under which the rain was collected can make a difference. For example, rain which falls during a sunny day can be used to bring joy, happiness, strength, and success. Rain collected during a grey day can be used in magic concerning reflection and finding balance. Generally, rain water makes a great go-to and can be used in pretty much every type of magical working.

Sea Water

The sea is most often seen as a precursor to life, and appears in many creation myths throughout the world. Often referred to as the primordial or primeval waters, these tales often begin with the world or universe being nothing but water. From this endless sea, deities spring forth, and create the world as we know it. These waters are often referred to as being dark and chaotic. As such, water in general but especially the sea, can represent the darker aspects of the self, and also creation and birth.

Sailing used to be of great importance to the ancient peoples. It allowed for trade, fishing, and conquering of new lands. Due to this reliance on traversing the seas, there are many tales steeped in folklore around fearsome sea creatures and sea deities. From sirens who would lull sailors to their deaths with their beauty and hypnotic song, to the large, squid-like creature known as the Kraken, there is no shortage of terrifying myths from most cultures.

The sea is one of the most versatile bodies of water when it comes to magic. It can be used to cleanse and purify thanks to its salt content. It can also be used to connect with water deities and the otherworld, and there are many myths and legends concerning otherworldly places which can only be reached by the sea. Take for example the Isles of the Blessed, where Greek warriors who had been reincarnated three times and lived pure lives in each would reside after their death. Or the island of Tír Tairngire, The Promised Land in Celtic mythology, an otherworldly paradise kept concealed by the cloak of invisibility of the sea God Manannán mac Lir.

The seas can also be used to heal, to connect with ancient wisdom and knowledge, to help us face our shadow selves, and to bring peace and balance. A lot of the tools that a water witch uses can be found in the sea, such as shells, mermaid purses, or animal parts.

If you don't have access to the sea, you can 'create' your own sea water by adding salt to water. This is great for cleansing tools and such, and saltwater is often used in healing.

Pond/Lake Water

One of the most famous tales involving ponds and lakes is the Arthurian legend of The Lady of the Lake. There are several stories which feature the powerful sorceress, but the most well-known is of her rising from the lake to gift the magical sword Excalibur to King Arthur.

I personally find ponds are a great place to connect with water spirits. However, there are also many tales to be found in folklore around the potential trouble some of these spirits can cause (and some of them are made out to be downright evil). Take the tale of Jenny Greenteeth for example. She is an old hag that haunts the waters around Lancashire, Cheshire and Shropshire in the UK. Also known as Ginny, Jenny Wicked o' Nell or Peg o' Nell, she hides in ponds and stagnant water. If children get too close then she will drag them down into the waters to either drown them or suck the meat from their bones. She very much fits the stereotypical witch trope in her appearance, with green skin, green teeth, long green hair, a thin face and large eyes. In some stories, she has no face at all.

As anyone who works with spirits will know, not all of

them are purely 'good' creatures. I will talk more about water
spirits in a later chapter, but ponds and lakes are great places
for work which involves talking to otherworldly beings, and
self-reflection. If you have some soul searching to do, or wish to
connect with creatures that walk in the otherworld, then staring
into the waters or making offerings is a great place to start.

Marsh Water

Water collected from a marsh has a real earthly association, and
is great for ancestor work, work to help you connect with ancient
wisdom and knowledge, 'dark' Gods and Goddesses, and death.
It is also associated with survival, adaptation, and working your
way through difficult situations. Banishing and protection spells
are also suitable for uses for marsh water.

Snow/Ice/Frost

Snow, ice, and frost can also help you connect with the energies
of water. Snow especially is associated with internal balance, so
collect some water from melted snow and keep it to use in spells
to bring balance.

Ice is great for freezing situations. If someone is gossiping
about you, or bringing negativity into your life, then obtain an
item associated with them (or write their name on a piece of
paper) and freeze it, to stop their behavior. On the opposite end
of the spectrum, if you wish to banish something, you could
write or draw it in the snow (or a symbolic representation
of it), and wait for it to melt. As it melts, whatever you have
banished should also melt from your life. This also works if
there is a situation which has become stagnant, or you have
become stuck in and want to make some progress. Or, if you
are trying to 'melt' someone's heart, maybe a colleague who for
some reason hasn't warmed to you. This can also be achieved
with frost, or by focusing your intent into a block of ice and
waiting for it to melt.

Dew

Dew, collected as the day is breaking, is often used in magic concerning beauty. Add it to face washes or beauty concoctions to enhance your internal and external beauty.

Well, Spring, and Fountain Water

When we think of famous 'fountains' many of us would first think of the fountain of youth. The Greek historian Herodotus wrote about it in the 5th century BC, and its legend has persisted throughout the ages. In the majority of these tales, the fountain of youth is a magical spring which restores youth to whoever drinks from it. One legend states that Spanish explorer and first Governor of Puerto Rico Juan Ponce de Leon was searching for the fountain of youth when he travelled to Florida, USA, in 1513. It was said that he had been told by Indigenous Americans that the fountain of youth could be found in Bimini Islands, in the Bahamas.

The element of water has long been known for its restorative and healing powers. It is often associated with the divine feminine, and of beauty. Add rose petals, jasmine flowers and lavender, along with rose quartz and moonstone crystals to a ritual bath or a wash to bring beauty and restoration. For an extra boost, seal it in a jar under the full moon to soak up the moon's power before adding it to your bath.

There is also the tradition of people throwing coins into fountains and making a wish; essentially you are making an offering and asking for something in return. Located in Singapore is the 'fountain of wealth', and it is said that if you walk around the fountain three times whilst constantly touching the water, you will have good luck.

In Rome, you can find 'La Fontanella degli Innamorati', or the fountain of love, situated next to the Trevi fountain. Legend has it that lovers who drink from this fountain will remain faithful and united forever.

One of the most well-known wells of the UK is the Chalice Wells in Glastonbury. Often considered to be a candidate for the earthly location of the sacred Avalon, the water from this spring is said to have powerful healing properties. I have used it in the past to pour around trees which have suffered damage to help them heal, as well as in rituals and washes to bring healing. Tokens and offerings are often left near the springs and petitions made, similar to the way we throw coins into a fountain.

Natural springs, and wells are again a great place to connect with spirits and otherworldly beings. If you have one local to you, go and sit or meditate by it, and try to connect with its energies.

Wells have traditionally been a source of healing, and appear prominently in myth and legend, and there are many deities associated with wells and springs. Well water can also be used to connect with the fae, and also to remove curses, or to curse another. There are several examples of clay tablets and such being engraved with petitions to remove curses, or to curse someone being thrown into wells and springs.

Collect well water to use in healing potions and tonics (if the water is safe to drink). Otherwise, it could be used to wash crystals or other charms that you want to use to bring health and healing. You can use it to banish any negative energy from you by focusing your intent into a bowl of well water, then throwing the water out onto the ground, and walking away to signify 'turning your back' on that which is bothering you.

River Water

One of the most well-known rivers in mythology is the Greek Styx – the river of the underworld. In fact, the Greek underworld had several rivers flowing to it, including the Acheron and the Lethe. Each river had a specific association with it, similar to the seven circles of hell. The Styx was associated with hatred, the Lethe was associated with forgetfulness, and Acheron was associated with pain and woe. There was also Phlegethon which was associated with fire, and Cocytus which was known as the river of wailing. Rivers have long been associated with transportation, both physical and spiritual, and often used in funeral rites. In Japan there is still held the annual Nagatoro Funadama Festival which is said to have started off as a festival dedicated to the water God, where prayers would be given for the safety of the boatmen on the Arakawa river.

River water is great for washing away negativity, and removing blockages. Many civilizations have used rivers to represent the passage from life to death, and in this sense, rivers are also associated with transformation. With rivers it is often the flowing motion of the water, rather than the water itself, that has the most powerful effect. However, if you don't have access to a river then using river water itself will suffice. Even a stone collected from a river will still hold the energy of the river and can be used in your practice.

If your intent is to speed up a situation or remove any obstacles that are preventing you from moving forward, grab a small branch and carve something into it which represents what it is you need to see some movement on. Focus on your intent as you do so, and then throw the stick into the river and watch as it washes downstream. Trust that as it flows, what is stuck will also become unstuck.

Similarly with banishing negativity, you can carve your intention into a stick and send it down the river, or you could create a herbal mixture using herbs associated with banishing and toss a handful of it into the river. Visualize the negativity being carried downstream and out of your life. Please keep an awareness when you are disposing of things into water; avoid plastics or any sort of container, and stick to natural products that won't harm the wildlife present.

You can also use it to pass messages onto your ancestors or loved ones you have lost. Again, take something natural such as a stone or a twig, and etch your message upon it (you may want to etch something symbolic, such as a heart for love), toss it into the river, and ask the spirits of the river to deliver your message.

Waterfall Water

Water collected from a waterfall, no matter how small the waterfall, can be used to enhance beauty, cleanse, purify, in rituals associated with birth, and in transformation.

If safe, add this water to beauty products to enhance your own beauty. You can also use it to cleanse and purify your tools or space, or add it to a ritual bath or use it as a wash to aid in transformation. Whilst it is also associated with birth, I would only recommend using this in rituals, and not in any way which involves drinking it or applying it to your body. Again, you never know what germs or bacteria are lurking in the water.

Crystal Water

Crystal water is water which has been infused with crystals. These are easy to make, and give us a bit more flexibility when using crystal energy. What you use the water for very much depends on the purpose of the crystal. You can also add oils and herbs to the water for an extra boost; I have a citrine crystal water with lemon and rosemary oil added to bring creativity, which I then use as a perfume when I need a creative boost. I also have a constant supply of clear quartz crystal water on the go, which I use to water my plants.

There are two ways of making crystal water. The first is called the 'direct' method, which simply involves leaving the crystal directly in water for 12 – 24 hours. However, it is worth noting that some crystals do not react well to water, and some can even be toxic, so please make sure you do your research if you plan on ingesting this water. If you are ever in doubt, then you can use the 'indirect' method. Place the crystal at the bottom of a glass, and then place another glass inside this glass, so that the crystal is trapped between the two. Then fill this second glass with water, and leave it for 12 – 24 hours.

There are unlimited uses for this water, so get creative, and have fun.

Herbal Waters

Similar to crystal water, this is water which is instead infused with herbs. Herbal teas are also included in this category. Again, similar to crystal water, what you use this water for very much depends on the herbs you use, and you can create one for any situation. Rose water is one very popular type of herbal water which is widely used. Be careful though; when boiling or steeping herbs in water, it can change the colour of the water. I have accidentally left brown stains on a white painted wall when creating a room cleansing spray before, so bear that in mind!

Moon Water

Moon water is water which has been charged under the light of the moon. It is most often charged under the full moon, but you can charge it under any phase of the moon. For example, if you want to use the water to help empower a new project, then you might prefer the new or waxing moon. You can use any type of water for moon water, such as rain water, or sea water, or even just tap water. Simply secure it in a glass jar (best to use a glass container with a lid) and leave it under the light of the moon for the night. This water can be used for many different purposes – cleansing, watering your plants, in ritual baths, or in any other water magic depending on the original association of the water.

Sun Water

This is basically in the same vein as moon water, but is instead charged in the sun. Sun water is great for any magic which involves God worship, strength, power, success, abundance, confidence, and happiness.

Many water witches will have bottles and bottles of different types of water – a water for every occasion! If you are collecting your own water, try to use glass containers rather than plastic. Toxins from the plastic can seep into the water and plastic is generally bad for the environment. Try to keep them in a cool area out of direct sunlight. As you can see from the list above, there are many different ways in which you can incorporate different waters to help you manifest your intent, so give them a go and see what works for you.

Where The Waters Meet

This is a combination of bodies of water, most often a river and the sea. Quite simply, these are places where two bodies of water meet and they can be places of real power. I have heard that these areas can be great for casting magic of confusion and chaos, but I personally see this union of waters as potential; the potential to create something new, to rise up from within ourselves and transform into whatever we desire to be. This is a place to wish and to pledge to your own success.

Not all of these places are places of positivity however. In my local county of Hertfordshire here in the UK, we have what are known as 'woe-waters'. Sir Henry Chauncy, author of *The Historical Antiquities of Hertfordshire* which was published in 1700 describes how the river Ver in Redford is joined by a small brook, and when this brook 'breaks forth' over the river, it is considered that death or some other calamity is on its way. Similarly, the Bourne Gutter which is situated in Berkhampsted is said to only flow when war is on the horizon.

Exercises

Think about the type of magic you usually perform, or the areas of your life where you may need some assistance. Do you work a busy job and feel the need to cleanse after a hard week? Or maybe you struggle to get up in the mornings and need something to help as a pick-me-up? Can you think of any of the above which could help you in these areas? For example, if relaxing and unwinding after a difficult day at work is something you need to do often, maybe designing a quick cleansing ritual which involves just washing your hands and third eye with sea water or rain water might help. If you struggle to wake up in the mornings, you could make some crystal water using a crystal renowned for its energizing properties to help, or maybe you could anoint yourself with sun oil to bring strength and motivation.

Once you have come up with a few ideas, then try them out and see how they work for you. If they don't work immediately, then try again or think of another method. With the various different types of water you can create, there are so many possibilities.

Ritual Baths

Ritual baths and showers are a very popular practice. A ritual bath is a bath which you have added herbs, crystals, and other objects to, to help manifest a specific intent.

Some people like myself don't have access to a bath and only have a shower. This doesn't mean you can't work this type of ritual; it just needs to be amended slightly.

If you do have access to a bath then the best way to start is to think about your intention. Then, collect the materials associated with your intent. Materials you can add directly to your bath are ideal, but if for whatever reason you can't then placing them around the edge of the bath will do. Herbs, crystals, candles, salt, charms, and other representations can all be useful additions to a ritual bath.

As you run your bath add each item and stir them into the water using your hand; stir the water clockwise to bring something towards you, and counter-clockwise to banish. Make sure you focus on your intent as you stir the water around.

Some people feel a bit funny about having a ritual bath to banish. As you will be bathing, the idea of sitting in water that you have been using to draw out negativity puts them off. I personally have never had any issues using ritual baths to remove negativity, but this is a personal choice.

Once your bath is run, take a moment to just ground and centre before you get in. Keep your intent in mind as you bathe and maybe even say a little incantation which aligns with what you aim to manifest. For example, when I am using a ritual bath to release negative energy, I will focus on whatever it is I want to release, and when I feel ready say *I release this – I let it go*. Make sure you bathe every inch of your body, including your face and hair.

Once you have finished with your bath, get out, and say a little thank you before you drain the water. You may wish to reaffirm your intention, such *as I am now cleansed, so mote it be*. Some recommend that you ditch the towel and let the air dry you but again, I have never had any issue using a towel to dry off after a ritual bath.

Ritual baths can be a bit messy so make sure you clean the bath well afterwards. If you want to minimize the amount of dried herbs and such sticking to the sides of your bathtub then you could place all of your herbs into a teabag or tea strainer and place this in the bath instead.

If you only have access to a shower there are several things you can do. Depending on your shower, you might be able to add all of your herbs, crystals, etc., to a cloth pouch and tie this over the shower head so the water flows through the pouch. In my experience this is quite difficult to achieve, so don't worry if your shower isn't quite right for this.

Another approach is to take those herbs, crystals, etc., and steep them in a bowl of water for an hour or so before you take your shower. Remember to infuse the water with your intent as you add the ingredients in the same way you would with a bath. Bring this bowl and a sponge with you into the shower and wash yourself with this water whilst you shower whilst focusing on your intent.

One of my favourite methods is to make and use your own soaps and scrubs to be able to use in the shower. These can also be used in a bath, but I find this especially useful not having access to a bath.

A soap can be easily made. You can buy pour and melt soaps from craft stores or online and make your own soap from scratch. Or you can buy an unscented bar of soap from the local shop and melt it using the double boiler method. Simply cut your soap up into small pieces, and add it to the bowl over a low heat. You need to add water to the soap to help it melt, so just pour in a little at a time – the more water you use, the thinner the soap will be. I tend to add my herbs at this point and stir it whilst I focus on my intent. However, be aware that this can turn your soap a funny colour, and so you may want to wait until the soap is cooling to add any herbs.

Once the soap has fully melted, pour the soap into a mould to set. You don't need anything fancy. I personally use plastic containers that sauces such as mango chutney come in when we order a takeaway! If you want to add any crystals, then add them at the point it is almost cool. This is also the best time to add any essential oils you wish to use to the soap.

This method of soap making is very quick – once the soap starts to melt, it only takes a couple of minutes, so can be done in a pinch.

Body scrubs are also easy to make, but need a bit more prep. You can use sugar or salt in your scrubs – sugar is gentler on the skin, but salt helps enhance that connection to water energies (especially sea salt). It is simply a case of pouring your salt and chosen herbs into a bowl and mixing them up together. Some recommend adding Epsom salt as it is softer on the skin – I personally have never had any issues just using sea salt or sugar but it might be worth adding if you do have sensitive skin.

I recommend adding a carrier oil or essential oil to the scrub to help bind it and make it easier to apply. Just use a small amount if you are using a carrier oil, especially if you have sensitive skin that is prone to outbreaks. You want to use enough that the salt and herbs start sticking together but can be separated easily and doesn't feel too greasy when you apply it. My go-to is virgin olive oil which is easy to find at most supermarkets or essential oil if I want a specific scent.

As always, no matter which method you are using, make sure the herbs, crystals, and any other materials you are using will not come to harm, or harm you, when added to water.

Exercise

Design your own ritual bath, or if you don't have access to a bath then create your own salt or scrub. All the ingredients you need can be purchased fairly cheaply from most supermarkets.

Working with the Tides and Astrology

We are often taught that the rise and fall of the tides are closely linked with the moon and its activities. However, the importance of the sun and its influence in this process is often understated. The tides rely on the gravitational pull from both the moon and the sun and a harmonious union between these two cosmic energies. I will go easy on the science, but essentially the sun has its own gravitational pull which interacts with the moons gravitational pull. This creates two different types of tides, the spring tide and the neap tide. Then within these two different tides, you get the high tides and low tides that most of us are familiar with.

Spring Tides: Spring tides occur when the moon and the sun are in alignment. As such, their gravitational pulls combine, pulling the seas in the same direction with great strength. This causes two extremes; the highest high tides, but also the lowest low tides. The moon and sun are together in this alignment roughly every full moon and new moon.

If a spring tide coincides with one of the equinoxes and the sun and moon are aligned with the equator, then we will experience the largest tidal ranges of the year. As such, it is a powerful time.

Neap Tides: Neap tides occur when the sun and moon are at right angles with one another. This means that their gravitational pulls partially cancel each other out. As such, we experience the smallest tidal range (less difference between high tides and low tides). In fact, the word 'neap' comes from the Anglo-Saxon and means 'without the power'. Neap tides occur during the two quarter moon phases (waxing and waning), roughly one week after the spring tide.

You can use the above to work out exactly which tide we are currently in, or you can search online. A lot of wild swimming clubs will post neap/spring tide tables (as they often encourage swimmers to avoid spring tides).

I personally love solar energy, and love incorporating it into my magic. Whilst the moon does have a stronger influence, I believe that our practice can become much stronger and more harmonious working with both solar and lunar energies, and not just lunar.

As well as the neap and spring tides, there are also high and low tides, and these can be compared in a sense to the phases of the moon. There are generally two high tides and two low tides over a period of 24 hours, and so roughly six hours between a high tide and a low tide. As soon as the tide rises to its highest point, it starts to lower again. However, similar in the way that you don't need to work full moon magic the very minute the moon hits full, you can give yourself a bit of leeway with the high and low tides.

The closer you live to the sea, or any river which is affected by the tides then the stronger you will feel a connection to them. I have found that proximity does make a difference which is a bit of a pain if you don't live close to the sea or suitable river. However, that shouldn't stop you from giving it a go and seeing if the energy of the tides affects you.

Low Tide: This is akin to the dark moon. This is when the energy of water is at its lowest, and is an ideal time for meditation, reflection, recuperation, and starting to plan the planting of seeds of preparation for any projects you have in the works.

Rising Tide: Akin to the waxing moon, this is a great time to build towards your goals and manifest what you desire. Use the rising tide to bring energy, motivation, and to work magic towards positive relationships, happiness, abundance, confidence, and anything you need to 'grow'.

High Tide: High tide is akin to the full moon. This is a great time to perform magic if you need something to manifest quickly, or to just generally bring more power to your workings. It is a time to acknowledge all you have achieved, and give thanks.

Falling Tide: Think of the falling tide as the waning moon. It is a great time to perform magic around banishing, removing negativity, and getting rid of bad habits from your life.

The Planetary Influences

Out of all of the sun signs, three are associated with the element of water; Cancer, Pisces, and Scorpio. Those under these signs may have more of a natural disposition towards the element of water, but this isn't a given. I'm an Aries, which is governed by the element of fire but I feel more comfortable with water which is its polar opposite.

There are also several planets which are associated with the element of water. The one which many witches tend to work with is the moon, and the moon rules the sun sign of Cancer.

Neptune rules the sun sign Pisces, whilst Pluto rules Scorpio. As such, these planets are also associated with the element of water.

The planet Venus is also one which could be associated with the element of water. Traditionally it is associated with both the elements of earth and water. Its traits of love, beauty, and the arts make it a good candidate for association with the element of water. However, bear in mind that Venus is also known as possibly the most dangerous planet in our solar system, often described as hot and hellish, making it a good candidate for the element of fire.

I personally don't work much with cosmology, but if you are inclined to use the planets in your magic then you can plan your work around the alignments of these planets to help further that connection to the element of water. Below is just a brief overview of those planets and what they represent:

The Moon: Femininity, emotions, relationships, memories, the home, motherhood, cycles, anxiety, fickleness, forgetfulness, divination, dreams, psychic ability and intuition.

Neptune: Mystery, spirituality, other worlds, connection, illusion.

Pluto: The unseen, the unknown, transformation, shadow selves.

Venus: Love, beauty, comfort, socialness, diplomacy, charm, luxury, fulfilment, the arts, vanity, greediness.

Exercises

Find out how far the nearest sea line or river large enough to measure tides is from your location. Even if it is far, have a go at meditating during high tide, low tide, falling tide, and rising tide and seeing if you can connect with this energy. If you are close enough to sense it, make a note of how it feels during these different periods. Are there any differences, and how could you incorporate these into your own magical workings?

Try the above during neap tides and spring tides too and see if you notice any difference in the energy, or your own energy, during high, rising, low, and falling tides for both of these periods.

It may be that you live too far away to fully be able to connect with them, and if you do then don't worry. You can still use the planetary influences in your work. Next time you want to perform any sort of magical working, take a look at the planet which might be best associated with your intent, and see where it currently is in the sky.

Chapter 7

Water Divination

The element of water is associated with intuition and divination. I associate most forms of divination with the water. Take tarot, for example; I will connect with water energies before performing a tarot reading to guide me, and then perform my reading. Lithomancy too is another form of divination that I associate with the element of water, even though it uses stones which are traditionally associated with the element of earth. With divination being associated with the element of water, you can use almost any form of divination and ask for water energies to guide you. There are so many different types to choose from, but I will just focus on three; water scrying, lithomancy, and reading with water animal themed oracle cards. Don't let this stop you from trying other forms of divination and finding one which works for you, or from using your intuition to guide you.

Water Scrying

Possibly the most obvious one. Before I took up water scrying (also known as 'hydromancy'), I had practiced crystal scrying, with varying results. However, from the first time I tried water scrying, it just clicked. The images and messages that came through were much stronger than anything I had experienced with crystal scrying, and it has become one of my favourite divination methods.

Scrying is the art of staring into something – most often a reflective surface – in order to induce visions of the past, present, or most commonly the future. Other forms of scrying rely on interpreting patterns created with whatever you are scrying with – for example, wax scrying. It has been practiced in one form or another through many different traditions and civilizations.

To perform water scrying you will need a bowl of water, or you could even use a body of water such as a lake or a pond. It can be any type of bowl you wish, although I personally find a bowl of a darker colour is best as it creates an illusion of depth, which can help induce the trance state necessary for scrying. I tend to use a small black cauldron when I am practicing this form of scrying.

How To Scry

Scrying is one of those practices that sounds quite difficult as it relies heavily on intuition rather than a tool. However, as with most things, practice makes perfect and this definitely is true of scrying. Even if you scry regularly, you will have days where it just doesn't seem to work. Simply stop, take some time out, and try again later. Below we will take a look at some key steps which will help you get to grips with scrying.

1. **Your tool:** In this case, the vessel you will be using to fill with water for your scrying. Once you have your tool, you will need to cleanse it. An ideal way to do this is 'washing' it with sea (or salt) water, whilst you say a little chant such as *I cleanse this object of all negativity, in this world and in all others.*

2. **Consider your environment:** Ideally you want to be somewhere comfortable where you won't be disturbed. I have mentioned reflective surfaces when it comes to scrying; this only works if you have a light source to shine off of that surface. I recommend dim lighting, maybe using a candle or a battery powered tea-light if necessary to provide the light you need to be able to scry by. It shouldn't be overpowering, just a little bit will do.

   You may also wish to burn some incense, or place

some crystals around you associated with divination to help strengthen your abilities.

3. **Make sure you are protected:** Visualising yourself in a protective white light is one tried and tested method, but it isn't the only one; you could use crystals or herbs designed to bring protection and keep them on you as you scry.

4. **Perform your divination:** As I've mentioned, scrying can be quite difficult for some and it takes practice. You may not see anything at all at first or even during the first few times, and that is OK. One of the most difficult things can be to just let go and let our subconscious guide us. Oftentimes, as we are reaching the state necessary for scrying or images start coming through, our conscious minds can fight to regain control. This is perfectly natural and one of the reasons that scrying can take some practice.

    Clear your mind; if thoughts start popping up, acknowledge them, and let them go. Stare into the water and let your eyes relax. Allow yourself to slip into a trance-like state as you stare, and wait for any images to come to you. I find that imagining myself going into the tool I am using helps, as if I am opening a door and stepping into the water itself.

    If you are scrying to receive answers or information about a specific situation, keep that in mind as you start, but feel free to let it go as you progress. If you try to keep this in mind for the whole session, your mind will be too occupied to slip into the trance-like state necessary for scrying.

    If you do see anything, it likely won't be straight away; be patient and keep going. I find that it usually takes anywhere between 10 and 15 minutes for images to start appearing.

5. **Interpret and record your results**: Remember, it is very unlikely that you will have a vision as it is portrayed in films and TV – a sequential, life-like rendition of the outcome of the situation you are scrying about. You will most likely see images, symbols, etc., that you will need to interpret.

   A lot of symbolism is personal; for example, one person may associate roses with love, but another may associate them with grief. So, think about what the symbols and images you saw mean to you on a personal level. If you get stuck, research the symbolism of whatever you saw and check a few resources to cross-analyse them rather than just taking the first meaning from the first resource you find.

   Make sure you record everything, even the images that don't make sense. They may make sense in hindsight. This can help in future scrying sessions and help you build up a personalized dictionary of symbolic meanings.

6. **Closing down:** I would recommend grounding and centring after any working, including divination. Once you have done this, turn the lights on slowly (if you turned them off) giving yourself time to adjust, and make sure you extinguish any candles, incense, etc.

Lithomancy

I have written a whole book on lithomancy, so I won't go too much into the detail of it here. Lithomancy is the art of casting stones and then interpreting the way in which the stones fall, and how the specific meanings of the stones relate to one another. Whilst lithomancy is traditionally performed with stones, I have one set which is made exclusively out of shells and pebbles I picked up whilst on a walk at the beach. I use this set when I have questions or queries which are primarily around my mental and emotional self. However, you can assign any meanings to the pebbles and shells in your lithomancy kit, and around any topic you want; you may want a set for general readings, a set specifically for love and relationships readings, etc.

You can have as many or as few shells in your lithomancy set as you want. Below is a small example set you can get started with if you want to give it a go yourself.

General Reading Set

- **Cockle Shell:** Represents happiness, joy, and new opportunity.
- **Clam Shell**: Represents love and harmony, and perhaps the need to 'make peace' with your situation before you can move on.
- **Limpet Shell:** Represents confidence, and the need to be able to overcome challenges, and let go of anything which doesn't serve you anymore.
- **Sea Glass**: Represents spiritual fulfilment.
- **Whelk Shell**: Dramatic change, or imagination and inspiration.
- **Black/dark coloured Pebble**: Represents a warning.
- **White/light coloured Pebble**: Represents that the universe is on your side, so go for it.
- **Any other shell/pebble**: To use as your personal stone.

To perform your reading, hold all the shells in your hands as you think on your question. Reach your arms out in front of you just below chest height. Move the stones around in your hands, not quite shaking them, until you feel ready. When the time feels right, open your hands and cast the stones in front of you. The shells which fall closest to the personal stone will be the most relevant or most important, whereas the ones which fall further out will be less so.

Let's say I have just been offered a new job and I am asking my set what will happen if I accept the job. I cast my stones and notice that the whelk shell falls closest to the personal stone, and the limpet shell falls close to the whelk shell. Just above the limpet shell we have the white pebble. We could interpret this as meaning that this new job will be quite a big change, and a challenge for which I will need to ensure I have the confidence to pursue. The limpet shell leading onto the white pebble symbolizes that this will ultimately work out for the best and I should embrace this challenge.

I have singled out lithomancy as it is the divination method I personally feel most comfortable with and I really feel connected with the element of water when I'm performing it. However, there is no reason why you couldn't instead draw runes or Ogham symbols onto shells or pebbles you have collected from the beach or near other bodies of water to use in other divination practices.

Oracle/Tarot Cards

There are many decks out there with a water theme when it comes to tarot and oracle cards. With divination being associated with the element of water, these types of decks always feel fitting. You can even make your own if you would prefer; I have created my own water animal themed oracle card set which works extremely well.

I have listed the cards and an overview of their meanings here should you wish to have a go at making your own. Simply find some card, cut out 15 smallish rectangles of the same shape and size, and decorate each with one of the animals below. As you decorate each one, keep the message of the card in mind to help imbue it with the energy of that message. Meditate with them also to help strengthen this, to make sure you receive the most accurate readings from your cards.

Octopus: The octopus brings spiritual guidance. It invites you to listen to and trust your intuition. It also represents illusion – maybe not all is as it seems.

Heron: The heron represents balance and the need to find it within yourself. It encourages you to proceed with dignity and a quiet determination.

Crab: The crab can appear when you are going through a period of emotional loss, and signifies that you may be feeling hurt. Take some time out for yourself first to heal.

Shark: The shark represents that it is time for action. Don't be afraid to create new opportunities for yourself.

Seahorse: The seahorse represents friendships, sociability, and finding joy through these.

Sea Turtle: The sea turtle represents going with the flow. Don't rush things; it is much better to take your time, enjoy what you are doing and get it right than to try and force a way forward.

Manatee: The manatee represents showing gratitude for what you have and living in the moment. Be open to new relationships and opportunities.

Orca: The orca represents creativity and empowerment. You are, or should be, using this time to undertake a journey of self-discovery.

Whale: The whale represents communication, especially when it comes to finding your own voice. Live your own truth.

Angel Fish: The angel fish represents unconditional love and acceptance – not just receiving it, but giving it too. Practice forgiveness and gratitude.

Coral: Coral symbolizes profound change. Trust in the universe to guide you through this change.

Lobster: The lobster represents independence. You may need to rely on yourself for a while, or perhaps a period of solitude is needed. It can also represent protection and the need to protect yourself through this period.

Piranha: The piranha represents that it is time to discover and celebrate your strengths and work on your weaknesses.

Seagull: When the seagull appears, it signifies a need to reflect on your own attitude and maybe adjust it if needed.

Salmon: The salmon represents perseverance. You may be going through a difficult time, but keep pushing – you are almost there.

Exercises

Are there any particular forms of divination which appeal to you? Maybe you already use one – can you feel how it may be connected to the energy of the water element, or how you may use the energy of this element to enhance your practice?

Before you next perform any divination, take a moment to connect with the water element energies and say a little prayer asking it to guide you in your reading. Perform your reading – did you notice any difference?

Have a go at water scrying, or perhaps building your own lithomancy set or water animal oracle card set and get practicing!

Chapter 8

Working with Animal Guides

Working with animal guides can be incredibly rewarding. They can bring you knowledge and guidance, help you overcome fears and difficult situations, and bring comfort. As the name suggests, they can guide us in both the physical world and the spiritual world, and each one has something slightly different to offer. Like deity work, working with animal guides is a two-way street; you will only get out of it what you put in. The more you work with your guide, the stronger your relationship, and the better they will serve you.

A guide may come to you for the moment and stay for only as long as it is needed. Other guides may stick around for longer. Either way, it is beneficial to build up a relationship with them.

Meditate with them and visit them regularly. Leave offerings, represent them on your altar (such as a small statue), and thank them when they help you. There is so much information out there on working with animal guides. However, to get started, take a look at the list below. Is there any one which 'calls' to you? Or maybe one has been calling to you for a while?

Oftentimes guides can make themselves known to us in the physical world. This can be a little trickier for the water witch – you aren't going to see a jellyfish just casually wandering down the street as you are on your way to the shops! However, you may find a certain animal popping into your head from time to time, or maybe pictures or references to them keep appearing. You may even dream of them.

You don't need to wait to be chosen by a guide. If you are on the lookout for a guide, try to pick one which either exhibits qualities that closely match your own, or ones that you wish to emulate in your own life.

Beaver: The beaver represents hard work and putting in the effort to make your dreams a reality. Think ahead, and don't give up. It also represents creativity, so could also be a sign to let go and indulge in your creative side a little more. The beaver also helps us to work harmoniously with others, whether that is friends, family, co-workers, or those in our community.

Crab: You may be experiencing issues when trying to achieve your personal goals. The Crab teaches us that sometimes we need to take a 'sideways' approach to things, rather than taking what seems the most straightforward path. It can represent inner reflection, and the need for a period of introspection and seclusion, a 'nomadic' approach, and the need for protection.

The Crab also represents balance, comfort, energy, freedom, mobility, movement, and the need to explore your curiosity. It symbolizes transformation, regeneration, success, prosperity, and status will be on the cards for you. It can also herald a rapid change, and issues revolving around trust.

Crocodile: The crocodile has two sides to it. On the one hand it represents strength, survival, and authority. One the other, it represents knowledge, wisdom, and healing. If the crocodile appears to you, look at the context it appears to you. For example, if it appears snapping its jaws, it may represent a warning that you need to protect yourself.

Dolphin: The Dolphin represents playfulness and joy, cooperation, peace, and harmony. It teaches us to follow our intuition as opposed to over-thinking everything. It can also represent balance, inner strength, protection, and resurrection.

Frog: The frog is often associated with transformation, the cycles of life, fertility, cleansing, and the afterlife. Frogs are also said to be messengers from deities and spirits, so if one appears then it may be that someone or something is trying to communicate with you.

Jellyfish: The Jellyfish represents acceptance, faith, and our emotional state. Sometimes it is necessary to just ride the difficult emotional times out rather than try and swim against them. You need to follow your heart; the journey may not necessarily be painless, but it will lead to growth.

Lobster: As a lobster grows, it sheds its shell, and often lives in seclusion. As such, the Lobster teaches us independence, the value of solitude, regeneration, protection of the physical, mental, and emotional selves, and waiting until the time is right to progress.

Octopus: The Octopus tells us that it is necessary to fly under the radar for a bit. Keep doing what you are doing, but keep it under wraps; this is not the time to make yourself centre of attention. It is best to wait until the last moment before you go public with your intentions.

Sometimes the Octopus can symbolize that you are putting on an act, or being someone that you are not. Sometimes this is necessary, but make sure you keep a sense of yourself if you do need to do so. The Octopus is adaptable, flexible, and also strategic in getting what it wants, helping us unlock our potential.

The Octopus is also associated with creativity, intelligence, and knowledge. It can bring focus and the will to succeed, especially in the face of complexity. It is an ideal guide to help you overcome obstacles using intelligence, efficiency, flexibility, and quick-thinking. If needed, it can also help you evade and defend yourself against that which may be troubling you. When the Octopus appears, beware of illusions and unpredictability. It is also associated with magic, mystery, power, movement, expansion, and diversity.

Orca: The Orca has many different associations. For starters, it is associated with emotions, balance, creativity, grace, harmony, empowerment, love, romance, personal discovery, sensitivity, community, and truth. It is also associated with many things 'mystical'; astral travel, alchemy, clairvoyance, dreams, intuition, spiritual insight, and past lives.

The Orca also represents creation, energy, family, freedom, longevity, perception, protection, strength, guidance/teaching, travel, truth, and vocal expression. As you can see, a creature with many associations!

Sea Horse: The Sea Horse tells us that we need to be persistent, but flexible. It is time to stop, and make sure you have an awareness of the situation around you before you make your move. Perception and perspective is importing. It also teaches us to go with the flow; there are some things that are out of our control, and fighting them is not worth the time or energy.

The Sea Horse also represents friendliness, generosity, contentment, patience, protection, sharing, and also parenting (especially fatherhood). It is often considered a good luck charm.

Sea Turtle: The Sea Turtle, unsurprisingly, is associated with the adage 'slow and steady wins the race'. It teaches us to appreciate the moment, to pace ourselves. It is associated with endurance, our sense of hearing, speed, survival, longevity, and patience.

Seal: The Seal represents becoming more aware of our imagination, insights, and inner voice. It tells us to listen to our thoughts and dreams, to channel that creativity and use it to progress in our goals. Change can lead to success.

The Seal also represents emotion, faithfulness, good luck, love, and understanding. It is a time for intuition, intelligence, and inquisitiveness. The Seal can also represent security, protection, and prosperity.

Shark: The Shark teaches us to take action, and create opportunities for ourselves. It is a symbol of authority, a God of the sea, which represents curiosity, power, efficiency, preparedness, protection, self-defence, and superiority. In a more negative light, it can also represent remorselessness, workaholic tendencies, and a resistance to change. It can be seen as a general warning.

The Shark is also often associated with innovation and inspiration, observation, the senses, movement, knowledge, perception and understanding, and suits those with a unique vision.

Starfish: The Starfish reminds us that the world isn't just black and white, and there is plenty of grey in between; often people's actions and words will fall in this grey area.

The Starfish is a symbol of hope, luck, and strength, especially in helping those who are recovering from trauma. It can help us form deeper connections, manage our emotions, and bring empathy. If you are looking for guidance, inspiration, and insight, then look to the Starfish. It is also associated with beauty, magic, light, the moon, perception, regeneration, and finding our path.

Whale: The Whale is known as a 'keeper of history', containing great wisdom. The Whale also represents communication, especially when it comes to listening to your own inner voice, and finding your own truth. It is also associated with physical and emotional healing, emotional rebirth, a peaceful strength, and helps us see the importance of family and community.

Water Birds

Albatross: The Albatross is a magical bird, and can act as a good spiritual guide, teacher, and messenger especially when it comes to path-working. It also represents the winds, weather, and the ocean probably more so than any other creature in this list. The Albatross is also associated with travel, independence, loyalty, courtship, and breaking through barriers and other limitations.

Cormorant: The Cormorant represents exploration and expression; not just in the physical world, but in our spiritual, mental, and emotional selves too. The Cormorant also acts as a messenger.

Heron: The Heron is one I feel close to; we have one which visits the pond up the road, and I often see it when going out for walks. The Heron represents dignity, tact, vigilance, and has a quiet determination and power behind it. It can help us with our self-esteem and teaches self-reliance, and can guide us on our life's path.

The Heron is also associated with transformation, wisdom, balance, boundaries, exploration, renewal, and the underworld.

Seagull: The Seagull represents taking a step back and viewing the situation from a different angle. More often than not, changing your attitude will resolve whatever issue you are facing. As such, it represents attitude, adaptability, communication, opportunity, perseverance, resourcefulness, responsibility, and stamina. The Seagull is cunning, but fair, and can act as a messenger when we need one. Other associations of the Seagull include freedom, friendship, joy, movement, and survival.

Journeying To Connect With an Animal Water Guide

Below is a simple journeying technique to help you find and connect with an animal guide. This can work in helping you find both a permanent or temporary guide. This journey will not just help you find that guide, but can be repeated whenever you want to visit them to ask for guidance.

You may find that a guide doesn't come to you right away. If this is the case, instead just try meditating to work out what is blocking you from making this connection. It could be a simple fact of feeling a bit tired and not in the right mind-set for meditation. Or it may be something more rooted in your subconscious, such as not feeling ready to build a relationship with a guide or you are trying to force a very specific guide to find you. You may find that as you meditate to break down these barriers, a guide appears to you here.

Water Animal Guide Journey

Make yourself comfortable and get ready for meditation however you usually would. When you feel ready, see yourself standing in a dark space. It could be a room, it could be a gigantic chamber, you can't tell – there is nothing but the darkness. Just spend a moment to feel yourself in this environment, in this darkness.

You see a pinpoint of light in front of you. You move towards it, and as you do the light grows brighter. You see that this light is coming from behind a large, stone door at the edge of this darkness. You reach the door, and pause. Acknowledge that once you pass through this door, you will be passing out of the earthly realm and when you feel ready, make your way through.

You find yourself stood in an estuary – the place where the freshwater of the rivers meets the salt water of the seas. Take in the scene before you; green marshlands dotted in front of you, with small rivers weaving through that lead down to the sea where the waters merge and become one. You can smell the salt water from here, hear the gentle rushing of the water as it winds through the marshland. You take a deep breath. How does it feel standing here, at the place where the waters meet?

One of these small rivers runs just beside you, and you follow it down towards the sea, carefully picking your way through the marshland. Tiny creatures dart beneath the waters, so small and quick they vanish almost as soon as you spot them. Focus on your intent as you follow the river – to find your animal guide.

You reach the place where the river meets the sea. A small patch of grassland with a large rock sits directly in front of the point where they meet, almost as if it was placed there especially for you. Sit upon this rock, and gaze back at the way you came and the freshwater that flows through the marshes. Then look ahead to the seas in front of you, stretching on towards the horizon, full of possibility and wonder. Take a moment to connect with this energy, and ask the waters to reveal to you your animal guide. It may come from the river, from the marsh, or from the sea, so keep an open mind and an open heart. What is the creature that appears? Do they bring any sort of message for you? Sometimes they appear just to bring us comfort rather than give advice. Sometimes they may not say anything at all, but just make themselves known to us. In some instances, you may feel the presence of something there, but whatever it is won't come forward. In these instances, thank your guide anyway and try again – it may be that you aren't quite ready yet.

When you feel done, reach into your pocket and pull out an offering to your guide. I find that shells work very well. Leave it for your guide, give your thanks, and promise you will return soon.

Stand up and walk back the way you came, to the door. When you feel ready, pass through the door and back into the darkened corridor. Move forward, upwards through the darkness, and visualize yourself moving upwards into your body. When you feel connected with your physical self, wriggle your fingers and toes and tell yourself *I am here, I am grounded, I am present.* Your journey is complete.

Exercise

Perform the meditation and see if any particular guide comes to you. If they do, do some research on that guide, and follow the steps in this chapter to start building a relationship with it. If you perform the meditation and nothing happens, don't worry!

Make a list of the qualities you need from an animal guide – are you looking for moral guidance, for something that will help you feel more motivation, more confident, etc.? Once you have worked this out you will be in a position to choose an animal guide which may best suit your needs. Again, follow the steps in this chapter to start building a relationship with it. Try to check in with your animal guide at least once every two weeks to help maintain that relationship.

Chapter 9

Working with Elementals and Water Spirits

There are many different types of water spirits across various mythologies, fairy tales, and local folklore. You may follow one specific path and so prefer to work with water spirits as they are portrayed in that particular tradition. If you consider yourself to be more eclectic, then you can choose the ones you feel most drawn to. However, if you are stuck with where to begin, then you can just start with honouring water spirits more generally. This is a perfectly valid approach, and if you are looking for something more specific then you may find that it reveals itself as you practice.

Working with water spirits can help strengthen our connection to water. They can also aid us and guide us, help to heal us, bring us knowledge and wisdom, and generally enrich our lives.

As a slight aside, one of the questions I have been asked is what is the difference between working with deities, water spirits, and animal guides, and why would you choose one over the other? It's an interesting question, and not one which has a definitive answer. My personal view on it is that deity is the 'highest power', and some form of deity has been around since the beginning of time. Working with deity allows us to experience a universal connection to all things and tap into wisdom and knowledge that has existed since time immemorial. Water spirits on the other hand aren't deities, but rather powerful beings that reside between the worlds. They are often tied to the land, and as such can help us strengthen a connection with not just our local environment but the otherworld also. Animal guides I personally see as having a stronger connection to this world than the otherworld (although we do sometimes work with them in the otherworld). Animal guides can help us with the connection we have to ourselves, helping us to learn and grow spiritually, mentally, and emotionally. So, there is a benefit to working with each – animal spirits on a more earthly 'personal' level, water spirits on a more otherworldly level, and deities on a universal level. However, this is just my take on it – there are many much more knowledgeable people out there who may have different ideas, so don't take my word as gospel!

Whilst pretty much everything I have written in this book is suitable for the absolute beginner, I do have to include a word of caution around working with water spirits. Water spirits are very enchanting. Some will promise you that they can grant you whatever your heart desires, and be quite intoxicating with their beauty and power. If you want to work with water spirits then you need to understand that they aren't all sunshine and rainbows, and be prepared. Here are some general rules I like to abide by when working with water spirits.

- Make sure you are protected. There are many good articles and books out there on magical protection. You could try crystals, herbal sachets, or protective sigils and symbols.
- Be respectful. The last thing you want to do is make a water spirit mad. Never use anything which may harm the environment if you are making offerings. Never demand anything from them. Never threaten them or try to bend them to your will.
- Do your research. If there is a particular water spirit you wish to work with, then make sure you do your due diligence.
- Remember, you should treat this as a relationship, and that means you have to give as well as take. Some water spirits I have worked with have needed offerings made before I try to work with them. It can take a while to build up this relationship and for you to prove that your

intentions can be trusted. If you don't want to put this effort in, then you won't receive anything in return.

They can also be tricksy, and certain types are known for having a penchant for taking and hiding belongings. When I first started working with a particular lake spirit, I found one morning that the shell necklace I wear as a tribute to my Goddess was missing from my bedside table where I always put it. I searched high and low for it. As I sat outside wondering where it could be I just got a feeling, like a little tugging at the back of my brain, and this spirit popped into my head. I told her that she could keep the necklace if she wanted as a token of the love and honour I have for her, but it is precious to me so I would really appreciate it if she could give it back. I left the garden, entered the house and went back upstairs, and as I entered my room there the necklace was just sitting on top of a pair of jeans. A place I had checked thoroughly at least twice! It could have been my dodgy eyesight, but there are plenty of tales of similar behaviour from the fae and such spirits.

I appreciate that some of that may sound like I am trying to dissuade you from working with water spirits, or that they are even a bit scary, but don't let it put you off. With research, practice, and a bit of common sense, I promise you that working with water spirits is very rewarding.

So how do you work with these beings? Honouring your local water spirits is a great way to start. At this stage you may not even have a specific spirit you want to work with in mind, but don't let that stop you. It is a great first step in building that relationship. Leave offerings near, or in, bodies of water if you can. I appreciate that not everyone has access to ponds or rivers, especially in the city, so you can always just make these offerings on your altar or a shrine if you want. What you offer is up to you, but remember to do your research if you are making an offer to a specific spirit to make sure you don't offer something which may cause offense.

Also ensure that whatever you offer won't harm the environment. One of my favourite offerings is water infused with flowers picked from the garden or whilst out on a walk and this is always well received. Try to make these regularly, and as you do so take the time to acknowledge and thank the water spirits for listening to you. You may even want to recite some poetry or similar. At this stage, we aren't asking for anything, rather laying the groundwork to build up this relationship. You may find after making a few offerings that a water spirit makes itself known to you, or that you begin to feel comfortable asking for something in return such as guidance or manifesting your desires. How far into leaving offerings you feel comfortable doing this is down to you, so listen to your intuition.

My personal go-to method when working with water spirits is through journeying. There are many different ways to try journeying, and that could be a whole book in itself. Journeying can help us contact and learn from these beings, and so if it is one method you want to try then I suggest you do plenty of research to make sure you are fully prepared. Starting off with animal guides is a great way to build yourself up to working with water spirits, so I recommend you try journeying to meet your animal guides first and foremost.

You could also use them in spell and ritual work. I have a ritual which I have written that invokes the nine sisters of Avalon for healing which I love performing.

Below are some different types of elementals and water spirits that you may wish to work with. I have gone ahead and just written about those that are relatively safe to work but this is by no means an exhaustive list. But remember, and I really can't stress this enough, do your research! Don't just pick a name from this book and start working with it. Instead, use this as a guide to set you down the path of working with water spirits. Also make sure to check your local resources too, such as museums or books, for information on your area. Many different places have tales and folklore specific to them revolving around ponds, rivers, wells, and the spirits of those places. The area in which I live has a fantastic local history society, and a ton of information about local practices and customs. For example, one of our tales features the 'Lady of the Moat'. It is said that on the eve of Valentine's Day, the ghost of the Lady of the Moat would arise from the moat which surrounds Moat Farm in Much Hadham. When she did, someone would die, often an unfortunate traveller just passing through. According to the tale she was murdered and her body thrown into the moat by her murderer, and she herself will continue to kill until her bones have been found and given a proper Christian burial. Whether there is any truth to the tale I do not know, but it is a great example of the local myths and legends that are out there if you have the time and resources to search for them.

The Nine Sisters of Avalon: These are some of my favourite water spirits to work with. Avalon is a sacred isle from Welsh mythology, and plays an important part in Arthurian legend. There are many amazing resources out there about Avalon from other witches who work with this blessed isle and the spirits that reside within it. It truly is a magical place that can help us heal, learn, and grow.

My favourite tale of Avalon comes from the 11th century *Vita Merlini*, where it is said that the Island is kept by nine sisters. The most famous of these is Morgen; whilst all of her sisters were considered to be great healers and shapeshifters who could even fly, Morgen was said to surpass them all. It is possible that this Morgen evolved into the sorceress we know today as Morgan Le Fay. Her eight sisters are only named once, and as far as I have found do not appear in any myths or tales after. Their names are Moronoe, Mazoe, Gliten, Glitonea, Gilton, Tyronoe, and then either Thiten and Thiton or two sisters both named Thitis. They are benevolent spirits and can be called upon to help heal, or to help you connect with the energies of Avalon.

Nymph: Taken from Greek mythology, there were two main types of nymph associated with water; the Naiads who were the nymphs of freshwater, and the Nereids who were nymphs of the sea. The Naiads were also broken down further into several different types; Crinaeae were the nymphs of fountains, Eleionomae were the nymphs of wetlands, Limnades were the nymphs of lakes, Pegaeae were the nymphs of springs, and Potameides were the nymphs of rivers. Often depicted as beautiful women, they were known as the personification of the land (or water) around them. They were beautiful, captivating, and with magical powers as evident in many tales. However, they were also fatally alluring, and could cause obsession, madness, and even death, especially among mortals.

Undine: Often interchanged with the nymph, the undine is one of the elementals most associated with the element of water. It was conceived of by the 16th Century philosopher and alchemist along with the other elemental representations – salamanders (fire), gnomes (earth, and sylphs (air). As he based these off of the work of the Greeks and their take on the four classical elements, undines are often considered a type of nymph. These elementals were not considered spirits, nor humans, but somewhere in between. Undines are physically very similar to humans and tend to eat and sleep, but are generally invisible to mortal eyes.

Siren: In Greek mythology sirens were creatures that would lull sailors to their deaths with their beautiful song. There have been many depictions of sirens. They were shown as birds with women's heads in early Greek art, and later on evolved to the form of a woman with the legs of a bird. In the 10th century the

Suda depicts them as having the form of a woman from the chest down, and the form of a sparrow from the chest up. It was in the 7th century that they were depicted as being women with fish tales in the *Liber Monstrorum*, and it is this depiction which has stuck. Whilst sirens are commonly believed to be female, originally there were both male and female sirens. As Greek art evolved, the male siren was removed and only females shown.

Mermaids: Depictions of creatures of human form from the torso upwards, and with fish tales where their legs should be have been recorded in mythology as far back as the Mesopotamian era. The Sumerian water God Enki has been described as having a body that was half-fish and half-goat, and images of a woman with the body of a fish and the head of a human can be found on coins associated with Demetrius III, King of Syria between 96 and 87 BC.

There is a wealth of information out there on mermaids, and I encourage you to have a look – you may be surprised. I personally have always been indifferent about mermaids (which feels kind of blasphemous for a water witch to say!). However, they have such a fascinating history that I really recommend you taking some time out to learn more about them. In some folklore they are seen as benevolent creatures who bestow gifts and healing, and in others they are seen as malicious creatures, intent on bringing death to those who meet them.

Selkies: Selkies appear in several different mythologies under different names, but the most common appear in Scottish folklore. They are seal folk, with the appearance of a seal and the ability to shapeshift into human form. Most tales surrounding selkies involve human men stealing the seal skin of female selkies when they are in human form and forcing them into marriage. However, more often than not when the selkie finds its skin it disappears into the ocean leaving her husband and children behind, longing to return to their watery homes. There are also male selkies who are said to be extremely beautiful and seductive to human women.

It has also been recorded that selkies are actually vessels for condemned souls or fallen angels, although this is not a commonly held belief. Like with most water spirits, there are also tales of selkies luring men into the seas who are never seen again. However, in more recent times they are seen as misunderstood creatures who are actually quite gentle and benevolent in their nature.

Melusine: Very similar to the mermaid, Melusine is a creature that can be found dwelling in freshwater rather than salt water. She is often depicted as having the tale of a serpent, or two fish tails instead of the one the mermaid has. Melusine is considered to come from European folklore. Rather than being a type of creature in the way mermaids are, Melusine is an individual in her own right. There are many different tales surrounding her. One tells how her fae mother Pressina married a mortal man on the condition that he was not to enter the chamber whilst she was 'lying in'. He broke this promise (although in some versions of the tale accidentally), and so Pressina took their children and fled to 'The Lost Island'. At the age of 15 Melusine and her two sisters enquired as to how they ended up living on The Lost Island, and when they found out about their fathers broken promise they sought revenge. They were ultimately punished by Pressina for their actions and Melusine was cursed to take the form of a serpent from the waist down every Saturday.

Lake Maidens: In Welsh folklore the Gwragedd Annwn are Tylwyth Teg (essentially the Welsh equivalent of fairies) that live beneath lakes and rivers. Writ Sikes, in his 1880 book *British Goblins: Welsh Folk-Lore, Fairy Mythology, Legends and Traditions*, describes them as 'elfin dames'. Crumlyn Lake in Briton Ferry,

Wales, is said to be a popular home for many of them. Tales surrounding them describe how they are great hosts, but do not abuse their hospitality for it can leave them bitter and resentful. They were also known to take mortal lovers, and it is believed that there are several old Welsh families descended from the Gwragedd Annwn.

Lady of the Lake: The Lady of the Lake is a specific Lake Maiden considered fae royalty, most commonly a Queen. Taken from Welsh mythology, mostly in tales which make up the Arthurian period, there is some debate as to whether The Lady of the Lake is one being, or a title held by several lake dwelling maidens. The tales surrounding the Lady of the Lake portray a complex character, one who is both benevolent to those she favours, but also power hungry and cruel. As an unnamed Lady of the Lake, she is identified as a member of the fae who raised Lancelot and his cousins and continued to help him as he took up the mantle of the white knight. However, in another tale she is referred to as Viviane, born a human whom Merlin falls in love with. She tells Merlin she will only give him her love if he teaches her magic, but eventually entraps him for the rest of days and takes a different lover. From my own experience I personally believe that these are different rather than the same Lady of the Lake, but again this character has a rich history that I encourage you to look into.

Exercises

Pick one or two water spirits to do more research on and learn everything you can about them. Can you think about how they may enhance your practice, or how you might work with them? Or would you prefer to start working with 'water spirits' more generally?

Before you start any sort of work with water spirits, make sure you have some form of protection on you, just in case. What will you use as your form of protection?

Do your research, and if you feel ready, meditate (as opposed to journeying to begin with) on one of these water spirits. Make an offering, and record your impressions. The first time I made an offering to the water spirits at a local pond (and I used 'water spirits' in general), there was definitely a presence and this feeling of being able to have whatever I wanted if I indulged the water spirits – they could make my heart's desires a reality. Whilst obviously extremely tempting, I remembered how seductive some water spirits can be to try and entrap you, so just said 'no thanks, enjoy the offering', and walked away. However, you may find that you don't really feel anything after making your first offering. That's OK, and can happen.

Chapter 10

The Water Witch and the Environment

Chances are if you are reading this book then you are already the sort who cares deeply for the environment. Sometimes it can feel hopeless, especially when you consider that (at the time of writing) it is just a small handful of companies that cause the most harm to our planet. However, even the tiniest of gestures can make a difference and bring us one step further towards global change. This can be especially true of the water witch. Our oceans are in crisis; plastic, pollution, overfishing, hunting, and the destruction of the ecological environments so many sea creatures rely on are taking their toll. Even on a more local level we can see the damage being done. Urbanisation and the constant need to build means that many of our green spaces, and along with them our ponds and other bodies of water, are being destroyed. Raw sewage is being pumped into our rivers and streams, and the wildlife at our beaches are becoming more distressed and, in some instances, physically harmed due to human intervention. It is our job to protect our seas, our ponds, our rivers, and to fight for them.

There are many things you can do – below is just a small list of ways you can help your local environment, and the wider world, but before I get into it, I have one thing I really want to emphasize: Do NOT throw anything that isn't already present in the waters. I've read books on witchcraft which have recommended putting your petition into a plastic container and throwing it into a river. I've seen books on witchcraft recommend pouring perfume into rivers because undines like pleasant scents. Please do not follow this advice. If you want to throw something into a river to help rid yourself of negativity, use a stick or a stone. If you want to give an offering to the undines, use a small vial of water which has had naturally grown rose petals steeped in it. Please stop and think about what you are offering and the potential harm it could have before you make it. Otherwise, here are some more ways in which you can help protect our natural waters:

- Try to limit your own water use. Keep the tap off when brushing your teeth, wait until you have a full load before doing the wash, only boil as much water as you need, etc.
- Donate or volunteer with a charity which focuses on the conservation of our waters, even one local to you. Many run local studies and observations you can get involved in, which are fun as well as helpful.
- Pick up litter from around your local ponds and other bodies of water; remember to never actually go into the water itself as there may be unseen dangers.
- Cut down on the amount of plastic you use. Plastics in the ocean are a huge issue so try and use reusable or biodegradable materials where you can.
- Don't pour chemicals and such down the sink. Try to find all natural cleaning products, drain unblockers, etc. Similarly, if you enjoy painting or other similar activities, don't wash your brushes and things in the sink. When acrylic paint interacts with water the chemicals separate, and these aren't able to be filtered by sewage plants and so end up in our rivers.
- Keep an eye on developments in your local area. If it looks like any planned development could impact the local environment, ponds, etc., then raise it with your local counsellor.
- Avoid using pesticides or other chemicals in your garden, as these can leach into the water in the soil. This also goes for paved areas; if you are working on your car for

example, put down some sheeting to catch any leaking fluids, as these can run down paved areas and into the ground or into drains.

Chapter 11

Spells and Rituals

Below are some spells, rituals, and recipes which I have written and performed that I thought I would share with you. Feel free to use these either word for word, or as a framework to create your own spells and such. I have only included the practical application of the spell/recipe itself, rather than opening or closing practices such as opening circles or calling quarters. Incorporate these however you usually would when working magic.

You will also notice that I have on the whole avoided using specific bodies of water. This is because they can be difficult to access, especially if you live inland, and I want to make these spells accessible to all. You can absolutely use specific types of water to strengthen each spell if you wish; for example, you could use sun water when making the success water. However, tap water will work well enough for these spells.

Hag Stone Home Protection Spell

For this spell you will need a hag stone. I have a huge one which sits by my front door which I found on the beach, but if you just have a small one you could hang it up by the door if you would prefer. You will also need to create some protection water, as well as a bowl of salt water and a cloth.

Protection Water Recipe:

- 1 part dried mistletoe
- 1 part dried frankincense
- 1 part dried sage
- 0.5 part black pepper
- 0.5 part bay leaves

Boil the frankincense, sage, bay leaves, and mistletoe over a low heat, using just enough water to cover the herbs for about 15 minutes. I tend to make extremely small batches and so will add the herbs to a strainer, boil the kettle, and then steep them as if I'm making a cup of tea until the water is cool (again, using just enough water to cover the strainer).

Once you have done this, grab your hag stone. First, cleanse the stone with the salt water whilst saying something to the effect of:

By the element of water I invoke the energy of the seas to cleanse this stone of all negativity in this world and in the astral. So mote it be.

Once you have done this, apply some of the protection water to the cloth. Start to clean the stone with the protection water whilst visualising it protecting your home from all negativity. See negativity (you could imagine it as a dark cloud) physically coming to your door and being repelled by the stone. When you feel ready, hold the stone up and say:

Element of water, grant this stone your protective energy, that it may repel all negativity and keep all within this house safe from all evil. May the blessings of the Goddess be bestowed upon this stone, and may it serve and protect all under this roof. So mote it be.

Place the stone by your front door, or whichever door is used most often. You can repeat this spell every few months to give it a bit of a boost if you wish, and you can also use the protection water on yourself or other objects you wish to enchant for protection.

Black Salt Protection Recipe

Salt is associated with the element of water, purification, and protection. Black salt in particular can pack quite a punch when it comes to protection. It is relatively simple to make, and once you have made it you can use it in any sort of protection spell. It could be sprinkled round the boundary of your house or in doorways to protect the home, can be added to protective sachets or to a small bottle worn around the neck to protect yourself.

You will need some regular salt (preferably sea salt), ash from incense or a fire pit, black pepper, some activated charcoal, and a pestle and mortar.

Add the salt to the pestle, followed by the black pepper and the ash and start to grind it altogether. Remember to keep your intention (protection) in mind. I like to chant whilst I do this to help keep me focused on my intent and to help raise energy. Something simple like:

With this salt I am protected, no harm can befall, spirits of protection I pray heed my call.

Once this is mixed in, start to add the charcoal a little bit at a time, until it turns black.

Once you have finished, hold it up and say:

I call upon the element of water, bless this salt with your protective energy, so that it may repel all negativity and keep all safe from evils that may cause us harm. May the blessings of the Goddess be bestowed upon this salt, and may it serve and protect all that it touches. So mote it be.

Bottle the salt and keep it in a cool, dry place, and use as needed.

Success Water

This water can be used wherever you need some luck in your life or success with a particular endeavour.

- 0.5 parts cinnamon
- 2 parts bay leaves
- 2 parts dandelion
- 1 part basil
- Water
- Vodka
- A few drops of citrus essential oil (less is more, and will depend on how much herb you use)

Boil the herbs over a low heat, using just enough water to cover the herbs for about 15 minutes. I tend to make extremely small batches and so I will add the herbs to a strainer, boil the kettle, and then steep them as if I'm making a cup of tea until the water is cool (again, using just enough water to cover the strainer). Once your water has cooled, add the vodka first; this will help to preserve it and ensure that the oil doesn't just sit on top of the water. I usually use roughly 1 tablespoon of vodka to 3 tablespoons of water. Finally, add the water, shake well, and leave to settle for a few hours.

Cockle Love Charm

The cockle shell is associated with love. This charm can help increase the amount of love in your life, and that includes increasing your own sense of self-love.

You will need two cockle shells of roughly equal size, the larger the better. You will also need some red thread to tie them together, or if that doesn't work for you then you can glue the two shells shut.

You will also need a couple of rose quartz chips, a couple of clear quartz chips, a small pinch of lavender, a small pinch of rose petals, and a small pinch of lemon balm. You only need really small quantities, and of course the size of the shells you are using will determine how small a quantity you need.

Hold each item and say the below as you place it in one half of the cockle shell:

Rose quartz to bring love
Clear quartz to empower this spell
Lavender to bring peace
Rose petals to bring beauty
Lemon balm to bring joy.

Place the other cockle shell on top so they create a little container, and fix them together with either the thread or the glue. When you are done, hold and meditate with the charm. See yourself happy and content, and loved, from friends and family and yourself. When you feel ready, affirm:

I am happy, I am content, I am loved by all. This charm brings love into my life and I will receive it with open arms. I am grateful, and will walk this path with love in my heart.

Carry the charm on you.

Cleansing Bath Salts/Shower Scrub

You can use these as either bath salts for a ritual bath, or as a body scrub if you only have access to a shower. I tend to use sea salt in my scrubs, but you can use sugar if you have sensitive skin as it is softer. Otherwise, you will need:

- 1 part rose petals
- 1 part lavender
- 0.5 parts sage
- A few drops of lavender oil

Mix your sea salt or sugar into a bowl with the sage, rose petals, and lavender. Focus on your intent, the intent of cleansing and riding yourself of all negativity. When you are done, start adding in the lavender oil a little bit at a time. You want just enough to bind it together but not so much it becomes oily. When you are done, hold the jar between your hands and affirm:

With these salts I am cleansed. All negativity will be removed, and I will be cleansed and rejuvenated. So mote it be.

Energising Bath Salts/Shower Scrub

Use exactly the same method above, but instead this time use:

- 1 part dried mint
- 1 part lemon verbena
- 0.5 parts lavender
- 1.5 parts eucalyptus leaf
- Olive oil to bind it together

You can amend the affirmation to something along the lines of:

With these salts I am energized. I will be filled with passion and enthusiasm, ready to face whatever comes my way. So mote it be.

Speed Up a Situation Ice Spell

This spell can help when there is something which is blocking progress, or if you are waiting on a decision. It works especially well when used to remove smaller blockages and inconveniences rather than large or more permanent issues – for those, you may wish to repeat this spell over a longer period. All you need is some ice and a bowl, but if you would like then you can also use representations of whatever your situation is to help you focus on your intent. For example, if you are waiting on a decision as to whether your offer has been accepted on a house, then you may want to have a door key present or a picture of the house. This isn't necessary though, and I have performed this spell successfully just using the ice and my own visualisation.

Place the bowl in the middle of the space you will be working in, with any items you have gathered around it. Place the ice in the bowl and wrap your hands around the bowl. Meditate on your situation; the ice will represent your problem, so you want to really focus on associating the ice with your situation. Say:

This ice represents [insert your situation here]
As it melts, so shall that which holds it back.
Any blockages shall be removed,
And a resolution will come soon
Begone all that stands in my way!
Bring me my answers without delay!

Meditate for a bit, and see any blockages melting away and progress finally being made on whatever it is you are casting this spell for. I personally like to repeat the chant over and over to help raise power and direct that towards my goal.

You don't need to wait for the ice to melt. When you feel you have done enough, you can just leave the ice to melt. Once it has you can simply pour it down the sink to dispose of it, or even just leave it to evaporate (I only use three or four ice cubes when I am performing this, and if I leave it overnight the water tends to have evaporated before I can pour it out).

You might also like

PAGAN PORTALS

THE ART OF
LITHOMANCY

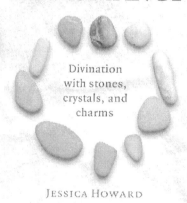

Divination
with stones,
crystals, and
charms

JESSICA HOWARD

Pagan Portals – The Art of Lithomancy
ISBN (paperback:) 978-1-78904-914-5
ISBN (e-book): 978-1-78904-915-2

MOON
BOOKS

PAGANISM & SHAMANISM

What is Paganism? A religion, a spirituality, an alternative belief system, nature worship? You can find support for all these definitions (and many more) in dictionaries, encyclopaedias, and text books of religion, but subscribe to any one and the truth will evade you. Above all Paganism is a creative pursuit, an encounter with reality, an exploration of meaning and an expression of the soul. Druids, Heathens, Wiccans and others, all contribute their insights and literary riches to the Pagan tradition. Moon Books invites you to begin or to deepen your own encounter, right here, right now.

If you have enjoyed this book, why not tell other readers by posting a review on your preferred book site.

Recent bestsellers from Moon Books are:

Journey to the Dark Goddess
How to Return to Your Soul
Jane Meredith
Discover the powerful secrets of the Dark Goddess and
transform your depression, grief and pain into healing
and integration.
Paperback: 978-1-84694-677-6 ebook: 978-1-78099-223-5

Shamanic Reiki
Expanded Ways of Working with Universal Life Force Energy
Llyn Roberts, Robert Levy
Shamanism and Reiki are each powerful ways of healing; together,
their power multiplies. *Shamanic Reiki* introduces techniques to
help healers and Reiki practitioners tap ancient healing wisdom.
Paperback: 978-1-84694-037-8 ebook: 978-1-84694-650-9

Pagan Portals – The Awen Alone
Walking the Path of the Solitary Druid
Joanna van der Hoeven
An introductory guide for the solitary Druid, *The Awen Alone* will
accompany you as you explore, and seek out your own place
within the natural world.
Paperback: 978-1-78279-547-6 ebook: 978-1-78279-546-9

A Kitchen Witch's World of Magical Herbs & Plants
Rachel Patterson
A journey into the magical world of herbs and plants, filled with
magical uses, folklore, history and practical magic. By popular
writer, blogger and kitchen witch, Tansy Firedragon.
Paperback: 978-1-78279-621-3 ebook: 978-1-78279-620-6

Naming the Goddess
Trevor Greenfield
Naming the Goddess is written by over eighty adherents and
scholars of Goddess and Goddess Spirituality.
Paperback: 978-1-78279-476-9 ebook: 978-1-78279-475-2

Shapeshifting into Higher Consciousness
Heal and Transform Yourself and Our World with Ancient
Shamanic and Modern Methods
Llyn Roberts
Ancient and modern methods that you can use every day to
transform yourself and make a positive difference in the world.
Paperback: 978-1-84694-843-5 ebook: 978-1-84694-844-2

Readers of ebooks can buy or view any of these bestsellers by
clicking on the live link in the title. Most titles are published in
paperback and as an ebook. Paperbacks are available in traditional
bookshops. Both print and ebook formats are available online.

Find more titles and sign up to our readers' newsletter at
http://www.johnhuntpublishing.com/paganism
Follow us on Facebook at https://www.facebook.com/MoonBooks
and Twitter at https://twitter.com/MoonBooksJHP